A
RISING
HOPE

FINDING PURPOSE THROUGH TRAGEDY

REBECCA SANFORD

A Rising Hope: Finding Purpose Through Tragedy
Copyright © 2022 by Rebecca Sanford

Published by Lucid Books in Houston, TX
www.LucidBooks.com

Scripture quotations marked (NIV) are taken from the Holy Bible, New International Version®, NIV®. Copyright ©1973, 1978, 1984, 2011 by Biblica, Inc.™ Used by permission of Zondervan. All rights reserved worldwide. www.zondervan.com The "NIV" and "New International Version" are trademarks registered in the United States Patent and Trademark Office by Biblica, Inc.™

The author has chosen to use the NIV translation when quoting the Bible throughout this story. The author understands that most of the story occurred well before the NIV was published, but all Bible verses related to this story were adjusted to provide consistency for the reader.

ISBN: 978-1-63296-539-4
eISBN: 978-1-63296-540-0

Special Sales: Most Lucid Books titles are available in special quantity discounts. Custom imprinting or excerpting can also be done to fit special needs. Contact Lucid Books at Info@LucidBooks.com

To Monique, who allowed me to see in real ways how God creates purpose out of our tragedies.

To all those I met along the way whose lives were transformed because they allowed God to create purpose out of their tragedies, especially after meeting Monique.

To the Nanny Monique Organization that is now operating through those whose lives were transformed by God under Monique's guidance. Her legacy lives on as hope continues to rise.

Table of Contents

Foreword

Monique Ladosz and I met in the summer of 2008. As I got to know her and what made her heart beat, she had a significant impact on my life. She shared her life experiences, and I thought her story needed to be told. I asked people who were writers if they would be interested in writing this story, but each time something prevented them from writing it.

Asking God who I could ask next to write the story, I sensed God saying to me that I was the one who should write it. But I am not a writer. Surely there was someone else who would do a better job than I could. A few days and prayers later, I humbly and timidly accepted the task. I decided to use my personal journal I had written every summer since 2008 as a starting point to tell Monique's story, the story of her ministry, and the stories of the people I met along the way in Uganda and Rwanda.

Each summer as Monique and I spent time together talking, she told me about the seasons of her life. I took notes and wrote a chapter or two, and then she corrected or added to the manuscript. One summer as we did some traveling together, we stopped in France and Switzerland to see where she had grown up, which gave me detailed information about her childhood in Europe.

I did the writing, but Monique told the stories and made the corrections. Nothing in this book was written without her approval. In the summer of 2020, Monique told me over the phone that she felt it was time to publish the book. She was ready even though the story held intimate details of her struggles, but it also told of her eventual redemption.

The world was in the middle of a global pandemic, and I never saw Monique again. She passed away that September. The book was put on hold as we all tried to make it through the pandemic, but it is now time to publish it. Monique's story and the stories of the people she ministered to in Uganda and Rwanda reveal the reality of a living God who lets us experience heaven on earth in tangible ways.

Preface

"Buy Ticket Now." Do I really want to push that button? The computer seems to be waiting for me in an impatient sort of way. What if I made this idea up in my head? What if it isn't what I think God is prompting me to do? This ticket is expensive! It's got to be one of the most expensive tickets you can buy. Who does that?

I slowly and hesitantly slide my pinky finger over to the enter button on the computer. Click. It's done! I'm going to Uganda to encourage a woman I don't even know . . . by myself! I have no idea of the adventure I will be on or the incredible people I am about to meet.

Introduction

This book is the result of my decision in 2008 to see what a particular ministry was doing in what I thought was just Uganda. That decision changed my life in many ways. Through my travels and relationships with these people, I saw firsthand how God can and does redeem lives. He is the one who picked them up and gave them the desires of their hearts. Then they were able to encourage others on this path of life. These were the people who went through things in their lives that to me seemed somewhat impossible for anyone to survive.

I saw with my own eyes how God helped those who lived a hellish life and overcame. When I first met these people, I could have never imagined what they had gone through. Once their stories began to unfold before me, I struggled to understand how they could have ever gone on. But God was the common thread that healed them and redeemed their lives. Did they have remnants of the hell they lived through? Yes, but God allowed them to rise from the ashes and make new lives. And here's the beautiful thing I witnessed. Not only did they soar like eagles, but they also reached out to others. These are the stories I feel compelled to tell, not just so you will be awed by them but so you will be awed by a God who can work in any life who yields to Him. I have witnessed His will being done on earth as it is in heaven.

This is my journey and interaction with people who the world will never notice or recognize on any grand scale. But God delights in them. And they are beautiful. The main thread is the story of the woman I went to visit in Uganda and got to know quite well. It is about the ministry she began in Uganda and Rwanda and operated for more than 30 years. As I learned about the aspects of the ministry, I became acquainted with her story—a story of many struggles and redemption. I have woven in many other stories of people I came to know over my 12 summers in Africa. They are all worth telling, and they will encourage anyone who is going through trials. I hope you are as encouraged by these stories as I was and will ultimately be in awe of a God who truly cares about each one of us.

CHAPTER ONE

A New Beginning

The chill of February had thoroughly worked its way through the air. One early morning I was thinking about when our daughter would be getting married in just a couple of months. On this typical Saturday morning, I was communing with God while the rest of the residents of the house slept in. My mind wandered through the details of the wedding, and I realized that by the following summer, both of our daughters would be married and finished with college. Then my husband, Tim, and I could save for retirement and cruises. Whoa! Really?

Is that how the rest of my life would play out? There's got to be more to this stage in life than that. Something occurred to me as my thoughts began to meander that now was my time to do something more altruistic and get more involved with what God was doing around the world. My parenting role was done, I had energy and excitement for what God was doing, and I desired to be used by God in ways I may not have thought of on my own.

And then this thought ran through my head: "Go encourage Monique." Who is Monique? It took me a bit to remember that Tim's Aunt Ferne had started a ministry in Uganda called Widow's Might in the early 1990s. I recalled reading about a woman who later went to help her with the ministry, but I had never met this woman named Monique. I wasn't sure what to do with this thought, so I tucked it deep inside and decided to revisit it later . . . just in case it really was from God.

* * * * *

Our daughter's wedding took place, I had finished my year of teaching school, and my summer had begun. I recalled a thought I had back in February. Hesitantly, I started tracking down information so I could contact Monique. I contacted Global Outreach International, the ministry that was overseeing Widow's Might, and they willingly gave me Monique's e-mail address. Typing a simple email, I asked if I could come to Uganda and see what this ministry was all about. I timidly clicked the send button, feeling like I had just opened a can of worms.

In a matter of days, I heard back from Monique. She was polite but not overly enthusiastic and encouraged me to come and check it out. Then the postscript read, "By the way, do you know a Tim Sanford? I just finished reading a book written by him." Tim is my husband. Wow! What are the chances? I interpreted those words to mean there might be a connection here after all.

* * * * *

A year later I was on a plane to Uganda. I felt excitement and a little uncertainty about what I would be doing for three weeks with someone I didn't know. Throughout the process of getting tickets and making arrangements, I never felt any hesitancy about going. After Tim and I prayed about the situation, we both knew this was something I needed to do. It seemed to be the next step for me in my life.

After 28 long hours of travel, I arrived in Entebbe, Uganda, at 10:00 at night. The travelers sluggishly removed themselves and their personal items from the plane. The customs officers seemed to be secretly hoping this was the final flight of the day. We were easily shuffled through the lines. It was my turn to go through passport checks and customs. With the stamp on my passport, it was time to start the journey, but once I passed through those glass doors, I didn't know the script to follow. No more signs were telling me what to do or where to go. I just hoped there was a woman—I presumed she would be in her early to mid-60s— waiting there for me. Before I left the United States, I did get a few hotel contacts in case the woman I was supposed to meet somehow didn't make the connection. The glass doors opened, and I saw an older woman standing there holding a sign with my name on it. She was smiling and waving. What a welcome relief! I quickened my pace and asked if she was Monique. She hugged me, and with that hug, my journey began.

CHAPTER TWO

The Setting for Widow's Might

This is Africa! As we left the airport, I got my first scent of Uganda. Something was burning in the air, but it was softened with the aroma of flowers, lake water, and the warm earth. I later found out the burning was the outdoor fires used to cook food. As we drove the short distance to the hotel, Monique talked to me as if we had been acquainted in the past. I found an immediate connection to her. She was warm, personable, and friendly. We stayed at a hotel in Entebbe, which was right on Lake Victoria. We settled into our hotel rooms, and I could finally rest. My simple room had a bed, a bathroom, and a mosquito net hanging over my bed. Geckos ran up and down the walls, and I saw a spider here and there. Climbing into bed, I arranged the net to cover all of it. It felt quite safe. I heard armed guards talking in low tones right outside my window. They were visiting while they were on duty, which gave me a strange sense of security. Feeling safe in such an unknown territory allowed me to sink into a travel-weary, contented slumber.

"Are you ready for breakfast?" It was Monique outside my door. Ready? I had been ready for more than an hour and a half. I had stayed in my room since I didn't quite know what to do, know what was culturally acceptable, or know if it was safe to walk alone around the complex. My alarm had gone off way too early, and my timing was all off. So, I stayed in my room and waited. Monique's voice was a welcome sound. I eagerly opened my door, and we walked together to my first Ugandan breakfast. It was very British in style, and we sat in an open-air room and began our friendship. As we ate our food and drank our tea, we started sharing about our lives and our connection with Widow's Might and Ferne Sanford, my husband's aunt.

After Ferne married my husband's uncle, John Sanford, they served as missionaries together in what is now Congo, formerly Zaire. Their entire married life was spent serving others in Africa. John was killed in a plane accident in the Congo in 1973, leaving Ferne a widow and alone in Africa. She had become used to living in Africa and stayed there to serve as a housemother at a school in Kenya. She often went back and forth between the United States and Africa.

Monique and I chatted about my family connections with Ferne and about family members we both knew. By this time in our conversation, we had finished our breakfast. The timid serving gal asked if we needed anything more. All the other guests had come and gone, and it was time for us to head to Jinja, Uganda, where the ministry was located. Our time had gone by quickly. I could tell that my three weeks would be intense and interesting. I was about to find out who Monique was. Throughout those next three weeks and years after, her life, the ministry, and the lives of many Africans began to unfold before me. I would be touched deeply by

Monique and the other people I would meet, and I would never be the same.

We packed our bags and loaded everything into Monique's 1994 Toyota Rav4. Life along Lake Victoria was very beautiful. Lush, green landscape, blooming flowers, and rich red soil were everywhere. Monique started the car, and we drove off. I got the sense that she knew her way around this part of the world. She drove away from Entebbe right into Kampala, Uganda's capital, and didn't seem to notice the change in the craziness. Intrepidly, she steered her way through the overcrowded streets, giving her opinion of others' driving abilities or the lack thereof, and continued telling me about life in Africa.

There were a couple of close incidents where we nearly lost the side mirrors on the car and when bicyclists or pedestrians crossed right in front of us even when there was no room between us and the overstuffed, swaying truck in front of us. No one seemed to pay attention to the traffic lights with turn-only arrows or red lights. If you could get through the traffic in Kampala without getting hurt or hurting anyone else, it was considered a successful drive through town. Looking over at me to see if I was doing okay, Monique asked if I was scared. It might have been the expression on my face or my silence as she continued to tell me about the ministry, but Monique picked up on it. She seemed perfectly comfortable with the driving scenario.

We made it through Kampala and were on our way to the sweet little town of Jinja which sits right on Lake Victoria and the Nile River. Lake Victoria is the second-largest freshwater lake in the world, and it is the size of Ireland. It is also where the mighty Nile River begins its water trek to the Mediterranean Sea. Lush, green fields of tea bushes took my breath away as we drove along the road. Winding along the road to Jinja, we passed through the Mabira Forest, a rainforest of coniferous and deciduous trees.

It was very dense with many colors of green. Some trees were flowering, and some nearly provided a canopy over the road. As we drove, we came up behind trucks piled high with bananas, and then the forest opened up to fields of tea bushes. I had to readjust my entire impression of Africa. This was not the picture of this continent that I had in my mind. We continued along the beautiful, little two-lane main road between Jinja and Kampala for about two hours, and already I had learned so much about the ministry of Widow's Might.

Arriving at the ministry in Jinja, I was immediately greeted by the Ugandan people who worked in the ministry's office who welcomed me with open arms. Their acts of hospitality described the word perfectly. They carried all my bags and asked if they could get me anything. These people were so gracious! The office was previously a home so there was a guest room where they put my things, and I began to settle in with my jet lag.

After I took a nap, we went into town and ran some errands for the ministry. This fifth-largest town in Uganda seemed like a step back in time. The red clay in the soil made for dirty, dusty streets. There were some vehicles, but most of the people rode bicycles or walked. Many people knew Monique and waved as we drove by. The children shouted *"Monzugu,"* an African word they call all white people. The smiles on the children's faces were precious. The poverty was not, but they didn't seem to notice that their situation was so extreme.

By the time we headed back to the ministry, it was dinnertime, and the staff had left for the day. Monique and I sat down to have a bite to eat. We cleaned up and began to visit. Because Uganda is so close to the equator, the amount of day and night is almost equal—12 hours of day and 12 hours of night year-round. The light was waning as the sun sank low in an orange sky. The mosquitoes began to buzz around, and we shut up the house and office. I could hear the neighbors visiting as they passed by the gated homes in the area. By now the guard had come to the property and paced or sat in a tree with his rifle slung over his shoulder.

The evening drifted by, and Monique asked me to speak to a widows' group at a gathering that would take place the next day. I didn't know what to expect, so I went to my room and prepared for what I would say to the group. As I read my Bible, the words of Christ reminded me of how precious we all are in His eyes. No matter the background, no matter the continent, no matter our personal histories, because of his love, he died for all humanity. I fell onto my bed and slept soundly to the sounds of an African night. I can still smell the fires burning in the Ugandans' stoves. I heard the light murmurs of the guard to the groundskeeper, and I listened to the fan as it circulated the warm air. I felt safe under my mosquito net and fell asleep in the sweet, peaceful night.

It was Saturday morning, and the time came to talk to a gathering of widows from Jinja's neighboring villages. We drove to the meeting at a local church where Monique was allowed to hold her meetings. Widow's Might had started these monthly meetings to encourage groups of widows. Because money began to decrease for the ministry, the monthly meetings had to be spread out to once a quarter. The women traveled as much as three to four hours to be encouraged by other widows and hear how God was working in other groups. The meetings were an emotional and mental refreshment for their souls.

As soon as we got out of the car, the women greeted us excitedly in their traditional voices. A high, shrill, staccato "yayayayayay-ayaya" erupted from a room full of Ugandan women. They seemed to regard Monique as a saint. She represented all the goodness in life to them. I felt a little overwhelmed as I looked around and saw the difficulties of life etched deeply into their faces. They smiled and wanted to touch me, hold my hand, or hug me. I smiled with some reservations. Who am I to speak into their lives? They had already spoken to me as I tried to wrap my brain and heart around those genuine smiles that graced their warped, scarred bodies. I quickly prayed that God would give me the words to speak since I felt that anything I had to say would sound shallow.

As the women began to settle in for what they would deem a day that restored their souls, I looked around at the 300-plus faces crowded into the small church. They were dressed in their Sunday best Gomesis, a traditional Ugandan dress named after a man who came and gave the people clothing. Some had shawls that were draped over nursing babies. Some were sitting in uncomfortable positions on the floor with just a woven mat to sit on. Monique told me that many times they would stay for three to four hours listening to her teach and speak words of truth to them. Just being there seemed to give them approval. They suddenly felt valued.

One of the head widows led the women in praise songs. Hearing them sing lifted me beyond our apparent differences, and I knew deep within that we are all God's daughters. I sensed that I was neither in Uganda nor America but in our heavenly Father's presence. It doesn't matter what we call the ground we walk on when we worship the same God.

Realizing it was time for me to speak, I pulled out my notes and tried to scan them, so I didn't sound too robotic. It was hard to see the notes I had handwritten on a small piece of paper. There were no lights since there was no electricity. As I looked out at their faces, I saw true beauty in their tired eyes. They didn't know how beautiful they were. I wanted to freeze the moment and take the time to look carefully at each woman's face. That I couldn't do. I needed to carry on even though I'm sure I looked very strange to them.

Later, Monique told me that several of the women were of the Islam faith. Some of the Muslim women had shared with her that they were not allowed to believe in this God for fear of what their families would do to them. Some had shared that they believed in their hearts but could not live any other way because of what their people would do to their children. It just amazed me to see these women continue on in their lives even with all their hardships. They did it because of their children. Standing in amazement, I marveled at how God had given and continued to give these women the ability to persevere in such difficulties.

* * * * *

Later in the evening, Monique told me what life is like for these Ugandan widows. There is no support from the government, and many of the widows were their husband's second, third, or even further down the line wife. That meant they were less in the eyes of their deceased husband's family and received less support. They were left to try to support their children in the after-effects of the AIDS virus. Leaning on Widow's Might helped them start their businesses and get them up and running, and then their children would be able to take over when their mother died and left them orphaned. As I listened to Monique's description of these women, it seemed hopeless. Life seemed like such a cold, harsh reality. Yet they carried on and persevered, putting one foot in front of the other. My introduction to this side of the world gave me much to think about and ponder.

CHAPTER THREE

Where Monique's Journey Began

The next day was Sunday, and as we drove to a place of worship, I noticed the people walking to their respective houses of worship. The men walked beside their wives with a carefree swagger, carrying their Bibles. The women kept the children in line and out of the dirt, away from traffic. Regardless of their social position, the women had to keep going. They took the brunt of everything that fell on the family, good or bad, and it was mostly bad. They were the ones who had to come up with the food to feed their children, clothes to send them to school, medicines to soothe malaria, and tears to comfort them when they were neglected or ignored. As I looked around the communities, there were very few men between the ages of 30 and 50. There weren't too many older men due to Idi Amin and AIDS. I realized these women were strong, tired, alone, and worn out, but they kept going.

Most Sundays were considered a day of rest when I was able to rest, nap, and journal. Later, Monique and I made a light dinner as the sun was setting. As the sun gently slipped out of the sky, we began to visit in the cooling temperatures. I was curious to hear about her life as well as the lives of those I had just begun to get to know in Uganda.

"Monique, I would love to hear about your own life. Were you a missionary kid raised in Africa?" I asked. It seemed that maybe I had heard that somewhere, or maybe it was just my own speculation.

"Oh my, no! I grew up in France," Monique answered. "That is why I have this strong French accent. I lived in France during the war—the Second World War, not the first. You know I am 77."

My eyes widened! I would have guessed her to be somewhere in her 60s. I had a hard time believing she was that old after seeing how much energy she had to run the ministry. Her story began to unfold as we sat sipping our tea and she spoke to me in her strong French accent.

* * * * *

Monique's father, Lucien Mayor, was born on May 24, 1903, and was from Échallens, Switzerland. Gritli Wagner, Monique's mother, was born on March 3, 1901, and was raised in Winterthur, Switzerland. The young couple met at a Bible school in Geneva in 1927. During their time in Bible school, they felt God calling them to France to work as evangelists. Shortly after they were married in 1928, they moved to Héricourt, France. Off they went as missionaries so Lucien could be a tentmaker evangelist. He sold textiles to support his new family. Their first child, Bernard, was born in 1929. Monique was their second child, born in 1931, and then there was Anne Marie in 1933 and later Jean Luc in 1938. The young family lived in Héricourt until the time Monique was old enough to start school. They moved to a town called Belfort, a larger town than Héricourt and not too far away.

Life started as a challenge for Monique. On February 14, 1931, Monique's mother delivered her—a weak, jaundiced, and very small baby girl—at home. The doctor said he didn't think the little girl would live. Later, at the age of three, Monique was in the hospital for jaundice. Throughout her life, she would deal with sicknesses, but she always seemed to bounce back. Even as a child, Monique was a fighter.

The Mayors had a church in their home, and people gathered there to hear Mr. Mayor preach. There always seemed to be other people around, and Lucien and Gritli were willing to help others. Monique's parents were often gone on evangelism trips, traveling for a week at a time. Near and dear to Lucien's heart were the Jewish people to whom he talked and taught about the tabernacle. While they traveled, the Mayors had other people watch their children.

Lucien Mayor's ancestors were originally from Spain. However, his family had moved to the town of Lausanne, Switzerland, which is the French-speaking side of Switzerland and borders Lake Geneva. In Monique's eyes, her father was very handsome, and he could do no wrong. Monique loved her father. He was very tender to the children, and they knew he loved them deeply. He was gone a lot because his work took him on the road in France much of the time.

The Mayors lived in Eastern France, and it wasn't always easy for Monique's parents. There were times when there wasn't enough food for the family. Monique remembered that these were the times that Lucien had the family pray to thank God for his provisions. Other times Lucien had to rig up hot water for their home with some kind of solar device. He didn't believe in letting others know of their needs and believed he needed to pray and ask the Lord to provide for his family. That impacted

Monique so much that she later found it hard to ask for things for the ministry.

Her father continued as an evangelist and worked to help the Jewish people. During the war, he helped get Jewish people to safe places where they could hide. There were times when he came home after some of these intense days and simply broke down. It was very intense and trying work. His children never knew what he was involved in when he went out to help others.

When Monique was about 15 years old, her father told her a story about an incident where he and some others went to rescue a family and help them get to a safe house. When they arrived at the home, they realized they were too late. The Germans had already been there. Her father and his team found the family sitting around their table no longer alive with their tongues nailed to the table.

"I still can't get the story out of my mind—the story my father told us and what we witnessed around us after the war," Monique shared. "So that's why when I came here to Africa I was not surprised about people's evil actions. Because I had heard stories of the Second World War when I was young, I realized human beings can be evil."

Gritli Wagner Mayor was from Switzerland. She was Swiss-German and very stern. She was also a perfectionist. She was quite resourceful in keeping all her children fed and clothed, and she raised them with a firm hand. She was a proper German and raised her children to be just like her. Their home had to be exceedingly clean all the time. Often people would drop by unannounced, and Mrs. Mayor would always have tea and some refreshments for them. She lived by the motto that you must be prepared at all times. Monique remembered her mother telling the kids many times to make sure everything is always taken care of before they left for the day. Always make your bed, she said, and make sure the toilet is clean enough to drink out of and the sink is clean enough to eat out of. Always make sure you are wearing clean underwear in case you are in an accident, she taught them, and Monique would giggle softly.

People in need came first to her mother. Monique remembered times when she was excited on her way home from school to tell her mother about her day. But when she got home, sometimes there were people there who needed to speak to her parents, and she would suddenly not feel that her news was that important. Reflecting, Monique said, "I had a good report card and I rushed home to show my mom that I was first in my class. When I arrived home to show her my report card, I heard voices in my home and knew there were visitors. The moment to go and tell my mother the news was dead, passed, and I couldn't barge in, so I went into my room and swallowed the situation. That was the way it was. You had to accept that it was the way it was, and you could never pierce or reach my mom."

Monique continued with more stories. "I remember another similar experience of trying to do the best you can, and my job that day was to clean the stove. I had to put my whole self into it because I knew it would be inspected piece by piece. So I made sure I did it right. And then I went on to do my homework in my room. I heard some scratching, and I opened my door because I could see into the kitchen. There was my mother leaning over the stove and redoing my job. I was so hurt, and I thought, well, you could never win. I could never reach her level of expectations.

"So hurt, and so discouraged, I decided I had to get out of there and apply my goodness to other places. I felt I couldn't breathe. I decided to grab some kind of bag—you know, we didn't have suitcases—and just leave. I just wanted to leave that place. I had no idea where I was going, I hadn't thought that far. Besides, in those days no one would ever agree to take in someone who ran away. I never left. My mom saw that I was trying to leave and told me to go to my room. I was really scared that she would come into the room and swat me. Later that evening, my father came home, and my mom told him I had insulted this house and was preparing to leave. My dad came into my room, didn't say anything, but put his arm around me, and said, 'You know how she is.' He sensed my frustration and let me know that it wasn't my fault, but that was just the way my mom was. My dad did not want to take sides, but he let me know that he understood how I was so hurt by my mom."

Monique expressed that the words her father spoke to her that day became very precious. He let her know that he was sensitive enough to understand her frustration. Monique began to realize that she was taking things personally when many of the issues weren't her issues at all. Throughout the years, she realized she took these things too personally because she was a sensitive person. To this day, Monique's first thought is to blame herself or think it's her fault in some way. She was slowly learning to look at all these situations in a more appropriate way.

"It's amazing how childhood experiences influence you even in your adult life," Monique reflected. "Whenever there is an issue that comes up here in Uganda or Rwanda, my first response is to see if I am to be blamed, when many times I had nothing to do with the issue at hand. I do believe that whatever happens to us in life, there will be a purpose for it later."

* * * * *

It was nearly midnight when Monique and I finished talking. My eyelids had become extremely heavy, yet I was completely intrigued with Monique's story. The morning would be coming soon, and much work needed to be done. I would need to wait to hear more of her story.

CHAPTER FOUR

Servants Like Lydia

The ministry office opened at 8:30 a.m. as the staff gathered for a devotional time and prayer. As we all gathered, someone read a passage from the Bible, and then we discussed it. We ended the time with prayer for each other, the ministry, and the needs of the widows and orphans. By 9:00 a.m., the office began to buzz with activity. People began coming in with their needs, hoping to find the help they needed through Widow's Might. Grandmothers came in with their grandchildren and asked if Widow's Might could help with uniforms so their grandchildren could go to school. There was a steady stream of people with a steady stream of requests. Monique dealt with them and had the staff deal with some as well. We worked until 4:00 p.m. and realized we hadn't stopped for lunch. "Some days are just like this," Monique explained. At 5:00 p.m., we closed things up and began to make dinner plans.

"Days like this are hard," Monique explained. "The ministry doesn't have the money to help all these people. There are so many requests. Some you question, and some are legitimate. Some requests just plain break your heart. It breaks my heart when I look in their eyes and tell them that we will take down their information and discuss it with the staff, and yet I know there is no money I can give them. I never say no to them right out because time after time there has been a story where a person comes in with a sincere need and my heart goes out to them, and we beg God to help this one or that one. The next day I will get an email from the headquarters in Mississippi explaining that a certain amount of money came in. Many times, it will be the exact amount that is needed for a particular case. God is so faithful, and I see it often, yet I still doubt when I look into those eyes day after day. There are many we don't help because we can't. I have learned to daily trust God to be the Great Provider for these people."

I realized that Monique literally walked daily with God and had to depend on Him constantly. It's a beautiful place to be yet very tiring. It seemed like doing intense workouts every day without taking time to rest and give your body a break or time to restore what you have worked on. How did Monique keep going? I was amazed as I watched her work and relate to people. She didn't mess around and was very businesslike while showing compassion, and the people she worked with had a great deal of respect and love for her. We sat down to visit as the room cooled off from the heat of the day. It was now time to pick up where Monique left off the night before.

"You know I used to be an accountant. I firmly believe we are expected to work hard. My philosophy for the ministry is like the Salvation Army—soup, soap, and salvation, in that order. The philosophy of the ministry is 'do not give them a fish; teach them to fish.' Many Africans want to learn, but they haven't been afforded the opportunity to learn and work. Some only want handouts. I have to screen the ones who come seeking help and decide if they are coming for a handout or if they genuinely want help and will work for it. I call those the ones who need a hand-up. I have been taken advantage of before, but I must keep pushing forward in case I do find ones who want genuine help. The ministry's slogan is 'help them help themselves.' We must teach them a skill so they can become independent and break the chain of asking for handouts to survive."

After dinner, Monique and I went for a walk. We walked the quiet roads of Jinja. It was very pleasant. Friendly people walked by greeting us sincerely. Older school children were on their way home. The sun was lowering, setting the tone for a gentle evening. We turned the corner of a road, and Monique pointed out a guesthouse where many American mission teams stay in the summer. As we walked by, Lydia waved us in. "Come have some tea with me" was all it took. We wandered over and climbed the stairs to the little studio apartment she had as the innkeeper. Previously, Lydia worked as a nurse for Global Outreach and their mobile clinic. She took medicine and supplies to people who lived in distant villages. The people would line up, and the nurses would examine them and give them what they needed.

Lydia was a sweet, sincere, caring woman. She welcomed us with the usual Ugandan greeting of hugging with right cheeks together, left cheeks, and then finishing with the right cheeks. As Monique introduced me to her, Lydia looked at me with great affection and asked, "Are you related to Ferne Sanford?" Lydia was very dear to me that day, and I've never forgotten her. She treated me as if we had known each other for years.

It was a delightful evening as Lydia shared the stories of her illnesses and her dependence on God. She shared with us the beauty of God and her dependence on and awe for him. What she felt for her Savior was deeply relevant. And the ginger tea she served was amazing. Lydia had grated the ginger root and cooked it with the tea leaves. Even though the evening was warm, the tea hit the spot. The evening continued as we encouraged each other with Scripture and prayers. Monique and I needed to get back home, so we graciously left Lydia.

That was the last time I saw her. Monique informed me that she died later that year. She seemed fairly young, but she had a lot of illnesses. Her life seemed short-lived and plagued with diseases, but she had a sincere love for and dependence on her Savior. It's a beautiful thing to know I will see Lydia again. I'm sure her sweet, serving spirit is serving Christ joyfully and that she is whole.

CHAPTER FIVE

Occupied France

We wandered back to the office and decided to visit some more. Promising not to stay up as late, Monique began to tell more stories of her childhood.

When the Mayors lived in France, it was beautiful at first. They had a nice house and managed on a small salary. Monique's mother stayed home while her father was away a lot. There were times when the family only had one potato to share between the four kids, but they had each other, and Monique's parents supplied that needed stability.

The times leading up to World War II were tenuous and strained. It was a dark and oppressive time for the people of France and all of Europe. Monique and her family were among those who had to live during this horrendous time in France. When Monique was in kindergarten, she saw a movie about how the Germans hated the French people. As children, they didn't understand or sense the tensions that were beginning to thicken in France. Overall, Monique and her siblings considered their childhood as normal as everyone else's, even though her parents were very strict and didn't have much in worldly possessions. Monique shared that she and her siblings were sheltered from the events of the world as most children were at the time.

"I remember the time when you would hear the air-raid sirens," Monique shared. "We would run down into the cellar and wait until the all-clear siren blared. This was just part of a normal day."

September 1939 started as a typical month. But soon, people were announcing over loudspeakers that the war had begun. The Mayors were foreigners, so they were instructed to inform the Red Cross that they were living in France as Swiss citizens. There was an expatriation program through the Red Cross to have all foreigners sent back to their countries. The Mayors thus declared to the government that they were Swiss citizens living in France.

The Germans had not yet come to France, but then the inevitable happened. Monique was just eight years old. An unsettled feeling came over her, but she did not know why she felt the way she did. Children were not expected to know or need to know what was going on. They simply were taught to obey. When the war broke out, Monique's parents were out of town. It was a very strange and uncertain time.

Shortly after the war broke out, the Germans marched into France. Monique's family was living in Belfort, France, at that time, and it became a Forbidden Zone. This *zone interdite* was one of two areas where the Germans established their military base in France. The Mayor family was now living in this zone, and the situation was very grim. Once the occupation began, schools closed. The children were told very little. People gathered around radios, but Monique didn't know what was going on in the world much less understand what it meant for her little eight-year-old world.

Across Europe, people in each country were expected to return to their own countries if they were living elsewhere when the war broke out. The borders were open so Swiss citizens could travel safely before any fighting started. This was particularly important so families could return to their country of citizenship. This caused a problem for the Mayor family. Although they could leave Belfort since they were Swiss citizens, Jean Luc, their baby, was staying in the Forbidden Zone with family friends who were French citizens. The opportunity came for the Mayors to leave France, but one-year-old Jean Luc was still with the French family who could not leave. Monique's parents could not retrieve their infant son, and they would not leave the country without Jean Luc.

The time came for all foreigners to leave, and the Mayors were unsure of what to do. They decided to send the children ahead to Switzerland, and they would come as soon as they had Jean Luc. In October 1939, Monique's father took Bernard, Monique, and Anne Marie to the train station. The Red Cross had a nurse's station there where they examined all passengers for tuberculosis before they boarded the train. When the nurses examined Monique and Anne Marie, they found that both of them were contaminated with tuberculosis. Being diagnosed with exposure to or contamination of tuberculosis meant the girls had to go to a place called a preventorium that focused on preventing the disease from spreading. The girls boarded the train with other children. They looked out the window to see their father waving goodbye.

Monique recalled, "I can still remember to this day what dress and coat I was wearing. My dad took us down to the train depot and put us on it. My little sister and I just did as we were told. We waved goodbye as our dad stood on the platform and our train rolled down the tracks away from all we knew. Our parents had to stay in France. Back then children didn't ask questions. My sister and I just obeyed the adults who were over us. It was a very confusing and hollow time."

Monique didn't remember how her older brother made it to Switzerland, but he was not there with the two girls. He possibly was put on another train since he had not been exposed to tuberculosis.

"I was only eight years old when this took place. It was a horrible time for us. We never knew when we would be able to see our parents again. Our parents promised to get us as soon as they could. They did not even know what the outcome would be. I think back to those days and wonder how they did it, leaving their children alone in Switzerland. Their faith in God was very real and strong because it had to be."

The war was on with the German occupation of France. After the older children went to Switzerland, conflicts began all across France. While the Mayors were waiting for Jean Luc, the house they lived in was hit by a bomb, taking out the corner of the house where the kitchen and bedrooms were. If the children had still been with their parents at the time of the bombing, they most likely would have been injured or killed. Mrs. Mayor was taken to the hospital due to trauma. She didn't have her infant son, three of her children had been sent to Switzerland, and her home had just been bombed. She was physically okay, but she suffered mentally, which landed her in a hospital.

On top of all that, Mr. Mayor was ordered to serve with the Swiss army. He had to sign up and would possibly need to leave quickly. Mrs. Mayor was still in the hospital and Jean Luc was still trapped in the Forbidden Zone. They both knew where their children were, but they could not get to them. The war had just torn this family apart, and the pressures were insurmountable.

* * * * *

I tried to understand what I had just heard. Because I have not lived through war times, I don't often hear stories of hometowns being occupied by an enemy or children being sent away from their parents for safekeeping during an occupation. Monique's life intrigued me and caused me to wonder how the events of her childhood helped set her up to do the work she was now doing later in her life. She could have run from those experiences and buried them with the past. Monique did not do that. Those experiences equipped her so she could be truly empathetic toward the people she served in Uganda and Rwanda.

CHAPTER SIX

Three Young Ugandan Men

Three young men came to the office one morning. They had taken their day off to walk to the ministry. Reserved and quiet, they timidly stood while Monique received them with hugs and introduced them to me. We visited with them, and then they told Monique that they were there because they had not received their certificates. They had finished a computer course in town, which the ministry had paid for. After finishing the course, these young men had opened their first shop in town to sell and repair computers. This was their first real job, and they wanted to hang up their certificates as proof they had received the training.

I could see that Monique was very frustrated. Her concern for these young men was evident as she reassured them that she would look into it personally. Neither of the young men had any family to counsel them, so they came to Monique. These young and inexperienced men were very humble and polite while Monique counseled them in many areas. It was evident that Monique had poured a lot of love and work into these young men, and they had a lot of respect for her because they knew she genuinely cared for them. She didn't go easy on them, and they seemed to thrive on her discipline and love. They knew their lives had hope and a future because of "Nanny Monique."

Later that week, Monique addressed the director of the technical school and worked out the problem. Orphans were easily taken advantage of except the ones under Monique's care. She got things done.

After the young men left, Monique explained their situation to me. These young men were orphaned, and Monique had known their mothers who had been part of a widow's group through Widow's Might. Using ministry money to help train these young men, she had sent them to computer repair school, and then the ministry had helped them set up a computer repair shop in town.

Monique was the only advocate they had. Now Monique was fighting for these young men again. She went to the leader of the school and spoke with him. After a bit of a struggle, Monique made sure the boys received their certificates.

In many of these cultures, the orphan is not valued, and many people take advantage of them. But Monique was one person they did not want to reckon with. The people in the community knew that she would fight for the orphans and would do what it took to make sure her orphans were treated with respect.

Later, Monique continued telling me the story of these young men. "Their mothers had all died of AIDS. I knew the mother of one of the boys, and as she lay dying, she asked me to look after her son. What was I to do? I couldn't just leave him helpless. After his mother passed away, I sent the three boys to a one-year technical school here in town. They worked hard and completed the course. Just this last week, they opened a computer store in town. We'll have to go see it."

As we drove up to the computer shop, the young men were standing there with huge ear-to-ear smiles. We got out of the car and walked up to the shop where they hugged us and excitedly welcomed us. Their computer shop had a front counter and a few things in stock ready to sell, and they also serviced computers. There was a small table in the back where they were able to work on computers if a customer needed assistance. These young men were so excited about their business. Before Monique helped them, they were simply orphans without hope or a future. Now they were business owners. Their smiles expressed a beautiful ending to a sad beginning. These young men will not go without their share of hardships, quarrels, setbacks, and anything else that seems overly discouraging to us, but they were given a chance in life.

One year after they opened the store, they had some dishonest dealings they needed to sort through. Monique was always there to "set them straight." Since these young men had no one to invest in them after their mothers died, they struggled in many ways. Monique cared for them and saw their potential.

We all need someone to believe in us, to be a champion for us, and Monique was that to many widows and young adults in Uganda and Rwanda. Using what God had equipped her with throughout her life, she came alongside others who needed someone to believe in them. I am sure that without her wisdom, care, and toughness, many of these people would have had nothing.

CHAPTER SEVEN

Living an Orphaned Life

A few days later, I longed to hear more of Monique's life as a child. We sat down after the day's work and resumed where she had left off about her life when the war began.

The train that carried the two Mayor girls away from their parents eventually arrived in Geneva, Switzerland. Once at the train station, children were divided into groups by age. Because the girls had been exposed to tuberculosis, they were transported to a preventorium, a specialized place to treat people exposed to tuberculosis so they would not get the disease. This journey up the mountain took an hour and a half. Once there, Monique and Anne Marie were separated because of their ages and taken to separate rooms with many beds. They were given clothes that seemed like prisoners' clothes and shown to their beds. Both girls felt very alone and wondered if they would ever see their parents again.

Throughout the nights, Anne Marie cried out for her mother, snuck into Monique's room, and crawled into bed with her. When a nurse came by, she would grab Anne Marie out of Monique's bed, hit Monique, and scream at the girls for doing that. They were told that if they cried, the nurse would have to spank them. Then the nurse swiftly took Anne Marie back to her own bed. There were many cold, lonely, tear-filled nights. No one ever explained anything to the children, which left them filled with anxiety and uncertainty. They felt they had no choice but to obey orders and cry themselves to sleep.

The routines in the preventorium were quite rigorous. Bath time was every Saturday. The nurses lined up the children, stripped them down, and threw water on them as they walked through the "bath" room. Monique remembered them using a rough type of soap to scrub the children, and then they would rinse them and dry them off very roughly. The girls ended up staying in the preventorium for about a year. A year in the life of a child is a long time, especially when they had no word from their parents. Monique remembered that orphan feeling all too well. Both girls felt like orphans since they were alone and didn't know why they were transported to another country without their brother or parents. Monique explained, "When I look back on some of those times, the way the caretakers treated us would be considered abusive by today's standards."

Politics and war never make sense to a child. The Mayor children lived during a time when children just did as they were told and went where they were ordered to go. Monique shared that as a child her thinking was massively confused and nothing was ever sorted out.

After about a year in the preventorium, Anne Marie was admitted to the hospital with mastoiditis, an infection in the ear where the pus moves into the bone. Today, antibiotics would usually take care of this, but at that time antibiotics were not available. Monique had been having sinus infections and had to go to the clinic for a procedure that drained her sinuses. They swabbed the nasal passage to numb it and then inserted a tube and used a syringe to inject the medicine. She had 144 of these procedures to no avail.

It was now December 1942, and this time Monique's sinuses became infected, and she became very ill. Her sinuses were packed with pus. Infections were rarely controlled by medication, and surgeries were required to stop many types of infections. Usually, doctors had patients breathe a type of gas that put them out. But that did not work in Monique's case because of where the infection was located. So, the doctors localized the area by injecting needles into her face. They used a hammer and chisel, to go into her sinuses and break up the infection. The procedure to clean out her sinus canals lasted more than four hours.

Monique's problems didn't end there. The infection had gone into her ear bone, which was the same mastoiditis that Anne Marie had dealt with. The doctors pierced the abscess in hopes the pus would drain on its own. The plan was to operate the next morning if the piercing did not work. It worked! During the night the pus had drained, which was a miracle for Monique. This was one of the most painful things Monique remembered going through. It was also a very lonely time. No one came to see her the entire time she was in the hospital.

It was December 6 when Monique entered the hospital for the first surgery. Her recovery took place in December. She was in a children's ward with 12 filled beds. The food in hospitals is never very good, which only added to the discomfort of healing and being alone in the hospital. Breakfast was always porridge, and Monique had never liked porridge. There was one bright spot. Every morning, a French boy crawled under the beds from the other side of the room so the hospital staff would not discover him. His mission was to eat Monique's porridge, which made Monique and the boy very happy.

Not only was Monique recovering from surgery but she also had an allergic reaction to a brand-new medicine. It caused knots in her legs and made her skin extremely sensitive to touch. Walking became very difficult as well. The pain was so intense that the hospital staff put a metal cage over her legs so the sheets would not touch her legs. As a child, Christmas was a joyous time with family all around, but not this Christmas season.

Monique vividly remembered Christmas Eve when she was in the hospital. "The hospital staff wheeled me to the balcony edge so I could peer down into the reception area where they had a Christmas tree. I remember never feeling so alone, so outcast, so orphaned. My family was somewhere else, scattered, and I didn't know if I would ever see them again. It didn't help that I was not feeling well and it was during a holiday."

She was scheduled to be released around the time of her birthday in February, but her appendix flared up. On February 9, 1943, she had intense pain, so the hospital checked it out. She ended up having another surgery. The doctors removed her appendix, which relieved the pain that had been doubling her over. Instead of stitches, they clamped her skin so it would close as it healed. Monique's birthday was on February 14, and she was once again in the hospital, alone on her 12th birthday. To ensure healing, she had to stay another month before she could go live with a family. Monique would live in a home where two women took in missionary children. She didn't know where her sister was, and she had lost track of Bernard, her brother, as well. She was alone once again and feeling very lost.

Monique did only what she knew to do as a child—cry and carry on. The children in her new home attended school down the street and functioned as best as they could. One bright spot was when Monique found out her brother was living in the house next to her. Finally, she would be with one sibling. Knowing her brother was in the same town and right next door brought some comfort to her. However, they were not allowed to communicate because the caretakers followed a very strict form of religion that forbade girls and boys from talking to each other. It also didn't help that Monique was shy and always did what the authorities expected her to do. They had no other choice but to continue functioning as best they could.

Facing disappointment over and over again can be tragic in a child's social-emotional development. Monique thought life was difficult for everyone at that time. During her time in this home, the two women often read Romans 8:28: "And we know that in all things God works for the good of those who love him." Monique learned this verse as a child, but it didn't seem to have any impact on her young mind. It had been more than four years since she left France. Monique had spent 1,550 dark, dreary, long days away from her family, and all things were supposed to work together for good. At least that was what she was supposed to think.

Not all was dark and dreary, however. Monique went to camp in the mountains near Interlaken, Switzerland. After hearing some missionaries talk about the adventures of their work in Tibet, Monique began to have a heart for missions. The missionaries showed slides of people praying with the Tibetan prayer wheel and bringing food to the dead. Monique felt she needed to go and tell these people what she knew about God. Her faith was simple and childlike, but she told God she wanted to surrender her life to go where he wanted her to go. Little did she know what that would mean for her since she was only 12 years old.

Monique reflected on that dark time and said, "Now as I work with these orphans in Africa, I truly can relate to the feelings of abandonment. My story eventually worked for me, but at least I understand to a point what these precious kids have gone through.

I can see how my experiences in life have prepared me for this time and the people I now work with."

* * * * *

I would go to Rwanda to see Monique many summers. One summer before I headed to Rwanda, I asked Monique if we could travel to France and Switzerland so I could learn more about her childhood and adolescent years. We met at the Dulles International Airport in Washington, DC, and flew together to Geneva, Switzerland. There, we traveled to the places Monique had lived and sometimes stopped to have lunch or dinner with her friends and family members.

One woman's story really impacted me as she described what life was like during the war. Marie was a friend of the family, and she was 15 years old when the war finally ended. Her family had a home outside the city of Nancy, France, near the border of the Forbidden Zone where German soldiers came to fight and bomb the area. The family housed many people who needed a safe place to stay, people who would otherwise be killed by the Germans.

German soldiers went from house to house one day telling everyone to get out. And two of them came to Marie's home. Her mother spoke good German, and when they knocked on the door, she answered by asking the soldiers a question. "Where are we to go? We have old ladies and babies here. Where can we go?"

Marie was listening from a distance and was very scared. One soldier answered, "If you stay very quiet, maybe you will be all right. But if the other soldiers come, they will kill you."

Marie's mother responded, "If the Americans come, we will be all right."

"It doesn't matter, you will be killed by any soldier," replied the soldier.

"There is a higher power than any soldier, and if God wants us to die or live, it will be so. We trust in Him."

Marie's mother spoke very confidently. The second soldier told his comrade that maybe they should stay with this family!

During that time, German soldiers were always walking around, and bombs were continually being dropped in the area. At one point, there were 27 people in Marie's house while bombs were exploding outside. The people were scared and screaming and thought this was the end. Marie's father began to pray, and all the people became quiet. They had the sense that God was with them, and there was a feeling of peace even during the worst times.

Later on, the bombings stopped. Everyone thought this eerie silence was very strange. Then a young teenage girl came crawling to their house and knocked quietly on their door. She had an urgent message. "The Americans are coming!"

Marie and a few of her siblings crawled through the garden and headed to the road behind their property. The kids were always careful to never go into the ditches beside the roads because there could be mines there. They arrived at the road where the Americans were to come. What they saw caused them to just stare. They didn't feel any hope or excitement due to years of living with anguish.

Tanks and American soldiers were coming down the road! Marie went up to one of the soldiers, and as he chewed his gum, she told him there were German soldiers on the other side of their house. She could lead the American soldiers directly to them. To her dismay, he told Marie they had to follow orders and meet in a church not far from where they were. The teens were disappointed, and it seemed the Americans were not going to do anything for Marie's family.

After a while, things quieted down, but Marie's household was still very afraid. During this time, some of the American soldiers stayed with Marie's family. Some attended their church and got to know the family. As Marie's family got acquainted with these American soldiers, they considered them family.

Whenever there was a battle, the names of soldiers who were killed or wounded were announced in the town squares and churches. Some of the Americans Marie's family knew were sometimes on that list. One thing Marie and her family were never able to understand was why these young men were willing to give up their lives when they were not even fighting for their own country.

As Marie shared these stories with me, I could sense deep respect for those soldiers she had known. She went on to tell me that many French people were very grateful for the Americans, and they could not understand what would compel them to sacrifice their own lives for others.

These stories came from the world Monique grew up in. Those of us who have not had to live through war are far removed from those who have lived so differently than us. This glimpse into Monique's childhood helped me understand the work and ministry she was doing in Uganda and Rwanda.

CHAPTER EIGHT

More African Stories

A new day arrived, and we jumped into the joys and challenges as people walked through the door of Widow's Might. Many people came, asking for help. Monique had to decide which ones to help and who to turn away. It was very difficult because she never knew who was telling the entire truth. One young student in his 20s wanted help with university fees. We had to tell him there wasn't any money for that. After praying with him and encouraging him, Monique gave him some creative ideas on what he could do. It was hard to see him walk away with a look of dejection. Many of the African students took many years to finish school simply because they couldn't get the money to complete it in a four- or five-year time period. It was heart-wrenching to see these young men and women look so discouraged as if their hopes and dreams had just died.

A grandmother and two young boys also walked in and wanted to meet with Monique. The grandmother was dressed very nicely and had come to ask if Widow's Might would be able to pay for her grandsons' school fees. The parents of the boys had died of

AIDS, and the grandmother was left to raise them. About a year and a half after that meeting, Monique was able to get enough money to send the two boys to school. Those boys were able to attend school because of Widow's Might.

Every day Monique was presented with needs like these. She constantly had to decide who got what and how much. I don't know how she kept it up except through the power of prayer. Her prayers were like the strength that held up Moses's arms when God told him to keep them up during a battle. When Moses grew weak, others around him held his arms up for him (Exod. 17:11–12). After spending time with Monique, I realized she *must* have been relying on God. The people in Africa have few other resources or choices. Her dependence and trust in God were very real and evident every day of her life.

After a trying day, Monique wanted to show me around Jinja. We went to a restaurant right on the banks of the Nile River. We sat outside under a thatched umbrella drinking tea and watching the fishermen throw their nets in the water to catch fish. The simplicity and beauty that surrounded us were almost intoxicating. How could life in Africa be so contradictory with so much poverty and struggles and also such beauty and tranquility? Relaxing and taking in the stillness, we felt our spirits being renewed. God seemed to be saying, "I am bigger than all these problems. I care for these people as much as all the other people on this earth."

Watching Monique in this environment helped me realize how important it is to do what you can with what you have and then relax and enjoy what God has created. The burdens are too great for us to handle. It is important to rejuvenate the soul by surrounding yourself with nature and appreciating the culture and beauty of where you are. I appreciated how Monique lived this out whenever I came to Africa.

CHAPTER NINE

A Family Reunited

At the end of each day without ministry demands, the evenings found us in the stillness of the warm African nights. And Monique would continue with her personal story.

Eventually, Mr. Mayor returned for his children. What a day! Monique explained, "It felt like we had been redeemed! We knew our father loved and wanted us to be with him. We could be a family once again. Our mother did not come right away. She was ill and couldn't make the trip. I look back now and think that she must have had a nervous breakdown. My family lost everything in France. Our house was bombed, and we, along with everyone else, couldn't take anything out of France when we left. Who wouldn't break down during those horrible times?

"My father was ordered to join the Swiss Army during the German occupation of France and had to return to Switzerland. The Red Cross had contacted my dad and told him he needed to come and get his two older children. And my dad came and got Bernard and me. Anne Marie was in the hospital, and Jean Luc was still in France, stuck in the Forbidden Zone. My dad moved us to our family's hometown in Lausanne, Switzerland. He was able to get a small flat for us to live in. It was 1944, and I was 13 years of age."

As Monique's small family moved into the one-bedroom flat, they had only a small amount of clothing and one trunk. It was dinnertime, and Lucien had Bernard and Monique sit down around the trunk. There was no food. He told the children that they needed to pray and ask God to supply for them. Before they were finished praying, there was a knock on the door. Opening the door, Mr. Mayor found a man with cash in his hand. This man and his wife had gone to Bible school with the Mayors back in the 1920s. They had 10 children now and worked as tailors making uniforms for the Swiss Army. At the same time, Lucien was praying with Bernard and Monique, the wife mentioned to her husband that she felt they needed to give money to Lucien Mayor. The family had just gotten paid that day, so the husband, who had polio, limped all the way across town to give the money to Lucien. This family had no idea how desperate the Mayors were at that time. Monique remembered it vividly and recalled how those kinds of moments helped shape her heart and beliefs in her early years.

Mr. Mayor could not actively serve in the Swiss Army due to a previous heart condition. He did, however, begin working in the Army office just down the street from the little flat where they were beginning to put their family back together. Monique and her brother began attending school around the corner from their home.

In 1945, Mrs. Mayor, Jean Luc, and Anne Marie joined the family. They were whole once more. They moved to a larger flat in the same complex. Unfortunately, the children's lives had been so disrupted at such young ages that they struggled to connect with each other. Monique was too young to remember what a normal family was like, so now it was difficult to know what family was supposed to be like.

As the family tried to reconnect and start their lives over, they went on retreats and small vacations. Mrs. Mayor had inherited a small chalet in the mountains near Lausanne. Getting away from the busyness of life, the family enjoyed a bit of the scenery and solitude in the mountains. The little chalet was nestled in the mountains overlooking Lac Léman, also known as Lake Geneva. On a clear day, you could see Mont Blanc, the highest mountain in the Alps, in the distance. There were many good memories associated with the little chalet.

Woven in with the good times were trying times as well. Growing up is hard for any child, and Monique clearly remembered a moment when she was getting older when she wanted to feel grown-up. Her mother always made the girls wear their hair in braids. Monique thought that was a little girl's look, so as soon as she got past the gate every morning, out of her mother's view, she took out her braids and let her long, blonde hair fall down her back. She shared, "I was really feeling the part of the rebel, and I felt free and grown-up. I guess I was getting too confident with this practice of undoing my braids, and I happened to look back at the flat and saw my mom's face in the window looking straight at me. That ended my grown-up days."

The Mayors worked hard to raise their children in the admonition of the Lord. They attended church twice on Sundays and once on Wednesdays. The children were not allowed to play cards, dance, go to the movies, watch sports, or do any worldly things that would corrupt their young lives. Their parents were firm, strict, and used strong guidelines to raise their children. This was also a time of much disruption and confusion. Mr. and Mrs. Mayor had been married only 11 years when the war broke out. Their four children had been taken away, and they had no assurance that the family would ever be reunited. Six years later, they were reunited, and now they searched for what a normal, stable family life should be like. When they were all separated, the Mayors had a 10-year-old son, and now they had a 16-year-old son. Monique who was eight was now 14, and so on. This huge gap almost destroyed their family. Confusion and disruption had taken their toll.

Part of returning to normal was having the children learn to play musical instruments. Monique took piano and cello lessons and became a very skilled cellist. Her brother was skilled at the piano, and the other children also learned to play instruments. They tried to live a normal mid-1940s lifestyle in war-torn Europe.

There was a lot of confusion at that time, and families tried to put their lives back together as best they could. Monique remembered visiting their old home in Belfort, France, where they had lived before the war. They were reminded of the bomb that struck part of the house and the hand of God that had protected the children who weren't there at the time. Being separated didn't make much sense at the time, but now Monique could see how God had preserved them all.

Their lives eventually returned to a new normal. France was cleaning up the rubble and rebuilding, and the children continued with their schooling in Switzerland. Mr. and Mrs. Mayor were still doing the work they were involved in before the war except now they were ministering in Switzerland.

Rebuilding families, towns, and countries takes monumental work. Monique's family was no different. Life just moved on without any consideration of how each individual was doing. Looking back, children were not given the luxury of developing autonomy; they just did what was expected of them. That mindset helped Monique keep taking steps forward. The events in her life helped her understand what it is like to go through difficulties, and much later in life, she would fully realize the reason for those experiences.

CHAPTER TEN

Iris

In the work of ministry, every day greets you with different challenges and precious rewards. One aspect of Monique's ministry was working with widow groups and helping them with their projects. The widows in one particular group gave an account of their business. Widow's Might worked like a small microfinance organization. Any widow group that borrowed money to start a business was kept accountable. Many of these widow groups were able to support themselves through their businesses. Some owned a couple of cows, which was a sign of wealth. The ministry's mission statement was to equip these women so they could become independent and support themselves and their children. There were no handouts since that only kept people dependent and never able to rise above their poverty.

On one of my trips, I met Iris, a widow whose husband had been killed in the northern part of Uganda. She smiled, sang, and was very pleasant. Her smile lit up the room. You could tell wherever she was because she sang or hummed sweet, gentle songs as she worked. What made her so joyful even in her difficult circumstances? You could see the light of her Savior in her eyes.

As I got to know Iris, she told me about her family. She shared a picture of her children. The oldest was a teen. Then she told her story of how she was blessed to have a place to live. Her landlord was raising the rent, and she could not pay for it. There were days when she was living between two of the shops. "It was okay as long as it did not rain," she said with a smile. "We were safe, and no one hurt us." I'm sure a confused look came over my face. Living between two buildings? Really? Then she smiled even more broadly. "Monique has loaned me money to help pay for my new place. You must come and see it."

"I'd be honored to come to your home," I told her. I wanted to see her African home. After work one day, we walked to her home. It was about a 20-minute walk from the ministry house. We came to an area with some makeshift little farmers' market stands, which was close to where she lived. We turned down the side dirt road and entered an open area that was a shared space for the tenants to do their laundry, raise their chickens or pigs, cook their meals, and just sit and visit with each other. Walking over uneven ground with rocks and some cut stones, I had to be careful where I stepped so I would not cut my feet or stumble.

We arrived in front of her apartment, which looked like the outside of a storage unit. I waited as she unlocked the padlock on the wide, wooden door that was about 6' wide. She swung the door open to reveal her 15' x 10' home. She was beaming with pride. As we stepped in, I saw two cushioned chairs facing us. On the arm of one of the chairs was Iris's worn Bible. On the cement floor was a rug, and along the wall was a small cabinet where she stored her kitchen items. This was the front room. Behind the chairs was a curtain that Iris pulled back to reveal the bedroom. There was a double bed against the wall where two of her kids slept. There was another mattress on the floor where the oldest son slept, and then there was a mat that Iris unrolled every night to sleep on. The sleeping arrangements revealed how women are not as valued as males are in their culture.

At least there was no water on the floor, and the roof was covered with corrugated metal. She did her cooking outside over a little charcoal fire. She washed her dishes outside in a pan of water and stored them back in her house. I praised her for having such a clean place to live. We sat and visited, and she wished she had something to offer me to drink. Showing her excitement, she proclaimed that I was her first visitor. I felt honored. I actually felt good about her being in this place.

It began to get dark, so we prepared to leave. As we walked back to the road, she pointed out the public outhouse. I felt good about her home until I noticed the one small outhouse for maybe 40 people. And now in my heart, I wasn't okay with this. I wrestled with the contrast between Ugandan and American lives. I hugged her goodbye and felt the weight of how to balance this contrast. This was something I would continue to wrestle with for many years.

I think about the importance of being seen. Iris didn't care where I came from, and she sensed that I had seen her. Being seen gives value to a person's soul. So many times, we get caught up with outward appearances instead of seeing people with souls. Iris taught me that.

CHAPTER ELEVEN

Life after the War

Whether we were traveling to a ministry site or visiting in the evening hours, Monique continued her life story. She picked it up at the part when she was 15 or 16 years old when students were sent to English-speaking countries through an exchange program so they could learn English. A school in Glasgow, Scotland, was where Monique would go to learn the language. It was a struggle, but life was like that. Throughout Monique's life, she was expected to work hard for everything.

"It was a different time back then," she explained. "Now people seem to think that life is supposed to be easy and things in life are expected to fall in your lap. That wasn't how life was for us. My parents taught us to work hard for everything. I think that's why I can relate to these people in Africa."

As Monique boarded the train for this new endeavor in Scotland, she thought to herself that maybe she could be free, let her braids down, and maybe even wear some lipstick. The train traveled through the night and arrived in Paris first thing in the morning. Monique's parents knew that their friend, the gentleman who had brought them money that first night in Lausanne, was now living in Paris, and he agreed to meet Monique at the train station. Monique had about a day in Paris, so Mr. Martin took her to his home. They arrived in time to have breakfast and devotions. The verse that day was John 15:5 "Apart from me, you can do nothing." These words impacted Monique because she had always been a goody-two-shoes and wanted to break loose a bit. She thought this would be her chance. Right away she felt God was talking to her. She realized she didn't know where she would go to break loose. What would she do, and how would she break loose? Monique decided then that breaking loose was maybe not such a big deal. When her time in Paris ended, she boarded a train so she could board the ship to take her to London, England. She would stay in London with two elderly ladies and eventually make her way to Scotland to study English.

Monique studied for nine months in Scotland. She tried to study and master the language, but she didn't feel like she had a great handle on it, and she found it very difficult to understand their Scottish accent. The other students were not very friendly, and language school became another disappointing experience. She was also taking a correspondence class in corporate law, which gave her little time to enjoy life. And her lack of confidence kept her from enjoying anything on her own. Little did she know that learning English would come in handy someday.

After language school, she went back to Switzerland where her next life experience was about to unfold on her life's journey. Monique felt that life always seemed to be difficult. She grew up thinking that this is the way life is and always will be. Life continued for Monique as a challenge with a few happy moments scattered here and there.

Back in Lausanne, Monique was finishing up her secondary schooling. She had always been a very shy and quiet girl, and not much changed when she reached her adolescent years. At that time and especially for her family, teenagers had very limited associations with the opposite gender. She didn't know much about boys, and her parents never allowed her to be with them on a date or hang out with them as friends. During the recovery period after the war, the Mayors had a supportive group of friends they came to know well when they lived in France. One family who was especially good friends with the Mayors had a son, Pierre, who was six to eight years older than Monique. Pierre and Monique knew each other because of their families, but there was nothing more than just being acquainted with each other.

Back when they were children, Pierre had taught Monique to ride a bike when she was about seven years old. Unbeknownst to her, he had decided that he was going to marry her when she turned 18, which at that time would have been in about 11 years.

Once Monique finished secondary school and her student exchange program was completed, she moved to Nancy, France, in April 1948. She lived with a family friend who was Pierre's aunt. Monique was attending the university there, studying accounting. At that time, her parents started preparing to go to Brazil where Monique's aunt (her mother's sister) was ministering. After selling all their possessions, her parents lived here and there with various family members while they tried to raise funds for their next mission. They then enrolled at the Biblical Institute of Geneva for a few courses in preparation for the mission field.

While Monique was going to the university in Nancy, Pierre's family invited her to come along with them on some outings. There were concerts in the park that Pierre, his siblings, and Monique went to. They visited and simply enjoyed each other's company. November 7, 1948, was a cool and chilly evening while

Pierre and Monique were walking back from a concert. This was Pierre's chance to ask Monique to marry him, and he wanted an answer in a week.

Monique was not expecting a marriage proposal; in fact, she had no idea they were anything but friends. Monique recalled, "At the time, I thought this was very normal behavior for a marriage proposal. Like I said, I had nothing to base any of this off of." So, she thought this was the way a marriage proposal was done. "There was no thought to courtship or being in love. It was the coldest approach to a marriage proposal, like a bucket of ice. It seemed so abrupt. But I didn't know any different, and Pierre wanted to know my answer in a week. Not knowing what to do, I would consider his proposal."

Monique continued with her story. "So when the next week came on November 14, 1948, I said yes. I believed that when someone had prayed 10 years for this, it must be in God's plan. Since he had included me in his prayer for a wife for so long, I was sure it was God who had chosen me to be the answer to his 10-year prayer. And since I was so naïve, this whole thing was kind of a shock in a way. So I said yes. The circumstances felt it was almost forced because I would not think God would have someone pray for 10 years if he didn't have a plan for me to say yes. This time was not filled with emotion. It was more of asking, what is the plan? Now, what is next? I knew the Word of God said that he knows the plan he has for you. I figured I was now in the plan, at least for Pierre.

"Because I was still in shock about being engaged, I didn't tell my parents about our engagement until Christmas when I had moved back to Switzerland. Once I told them, they were excited for us since they knew Pierre's family so well. At that time, a young couple didn't plan a wedding but continued with their various schools and jobs for about a year. We were not able to see each other during that year. I was now in Bible school in Geneva, and Pierre was working in France. Our only form of communication was to write letters to each other, and since this was the plan that everyone else seemed to accept, I accepted the plan as well. I was going to marry Pierre.

"I was so afraid of being in love because then we would have to kiss. As I said, I was so naïve. Everyone seemed to be in favor of this union, and we had support from both sides of our families. A wedding just seems to cheer everyone up, and now I was the one who was going to have a wedding. I just went along with it, just like I had always been taught. Just do what seems right."

Much of life during the post-war period was learning to keep going. There wasn't time to think or plan things, especially for young women. Monique had been taught to do as she was told throughout her life, so it made sense to her to accept things in life without much thought to what she wanted. At the time, she was content with what was going on, and that contentment developed into what she understood at the time as love. Monique would be married in the very near future.

CHAPTER TWELVE

Her Name Means Star

The name Stella means star. This name fits a dear woman who had been with Widow's Might since 1992. When I was in Jinja, I was introduced to this beautiful woman who worked as an administrative assistant. When she heard my name, she looked at me with wide, inquisitive eyes. "Are you related to Ferne Sanford?"

"Yes, I am. My husband is Ferne's nephew," I replied. I could tell by her response to my words that Ferne had meant much to her.

Stella told me her story of how she came to Widow's Might in 1992. In 1990, Stella and her husband were living in Soroti, Uganda. The government had employed her husband as a soldier. When political tensions began to rise, her husband felt he could not go along with what was expected of him. He had gotten word that they were coming to kill him. He knew of nothing better to do than to take his family and literally run for their lives.

Stella, her husband, and their four young children were running away when the soldiers came and shot her husband. Stella kept running. She could not return to be by her husband when he lay dying. She continued running with the children. Many days later, they completed their 120-mile journey to the town of Jinja. She had a sister-in-law who lived there, and she planned on finding refuge with her.

Stella was exhausted, weary, and grieving but needed to continue caring for her children. The time with her sister-in-law was not easy, but Stella did the best she could. Two long years passed, and she and her children were still alive.

In 1992, a woman came knocking on her door to inquire about how she was doing. It was Ferne Sanford. A missionary in Jinja had given Ferne Stella's name. After finding out what Stella needed, Ferne began gathering the items she needed and started a relationship with Stella.

There was going to be a week of Christian outreach meetings in Jinja, and Ferne asked Stella to attend. Stella went and heard for the first time about the love and redemptive work of Christ. She had never heard that before. In April 1992, Stella gave her life to Christ.

She told me that she was so excited that she had to tell someone, so she told her children. At first, they didn't understand any of it, but through her excitement, they began to know the meaning of what their mother was talking about. Ferne helped Stella grow in her faith and helped her, as a young mother, care for her children without a husband.

Ferne needed someone to help in the Widow's Might office in Jinja, someone who would know the culture as well. Stella showed a lot of promise and began taking some office-skill classes. It wasn't long before she began working for Ferne in the Widow's Might office.

Ferne treated Stella and loved her as if she were her own daughter. That meant the world to Stella, and the two women grew close. Now Stella was able to care for her children, have her own place instead of living with her sister-in-law, and become a light to those around her.

Since 1992, Stella has worked for Widow's Might. The ministry's motto is help them help themselves. And Stella's life was a perfect example of that. She became skilled and capable even though she was a widow. Through the ministry, she was able to help herself and her children. Those children were able to go to school and receive an education, later marry, and have families of their own. Many orphaned children do not have the resources to go to school, and the cycle of poverty is repeated in the next generation. Because of Widow's Might, Stella, with God's help, broke the chain of poverty that widowhood casts onto so many of these widows. Ferne's obedience to God helped change Stella's life for the better, and God's love was played out on earth as he intended.

When Monique joined the ministry, Stella was there to help her adjust to Uganda. Their friendship and dependence grew into a deep and caring relationship. In the summer of 2018, I was able to attend Stella's wedding. Monique spoke during the ceremony of the deep friendship that had started so many years ago. What Ferne had nurtured continued to the end of Monique's life.

CHAPTER THIRTEEN

What Next?

Back to Monique's early story, Pierre and Monique made plans for their marriage and their future. They decided to head in the same direction as Monique's parents and serve God in Brazil. Maybe the hardships of growing up during wartime would prepare Monique to minister along with her husband as she had promised God when she was a child.

Monique enrolled in the same Bible school where her parents were taking classes in Geneva, Switzerland. It was now January 1950, and Pierre stayed in Nancy, France, where he worked. The couple wrote letters back and forth to each other for 18 months. Her parents were still taking classes, but there were strict rules at the school. One rule was that Monique was not allowed to communicate with her parents while attending the school. These strict rules never set well with Monique, but because she was shy and timid, she always followed them even when they did not make much sense to her. She had always been taught to do as she was told, and she lived in an era when no one seemed to challenge the authorities of any institution. Even though she complied with the rules, she was left feeling some frustration in not understanding the whys of the rules.

School continued for Monique. On her 20th birthday on February 14, 1951, some girls who were attending the Bible school began singing outside her door at 6:00 a.m. They were singing "I Surrender All." That song had impacted Monique when she was 12 years old and had decided to be a missionary. It seemed that all things pointed to being a missionary in Brazil with Pierre as her husband.

It was now May 1951, and Monique graduated from Bible school. She registered to become a nurse and started working in the maternity ward attached to the nursing school. At that time, Monique and Pierre did not have any specific wedding date, and Pierre was planning on attending Bible school so they could join Monique's parents in Brazil. But for some reason, Pierre was not accepted into the school. He immediately drove to Geneva to show Monique the letter of denial. It was now July 14, 1951, and Monique's parents encouraged the young couple to have the wedding in a couple of months on September 26. Mr. and Mrs. Mayor planned to leave for Brazil at the end of September, and Pierre and Monique could go to Brazil shortly after Monique's parents arrived. Little did they know how their lives were about to change.

"The wedding was about six weeks away when my world fell apart," Monique told me. "On August 4, 1951, I received a call from my dad. 'Monique, I have some bad news for you.' I knew right away it was about Pierre. 'Pierre has been in an accident.' 'Is it bad?' I asked. 'It's bad. As Pierre was driving home from work, he was in a fatal car accident.' When the news reached me, I felt like I was falling into a downward spiral. How could this be? Everything seemed so perfect! Instantly I became numb. I was in a fog or coma. I couldn't think, reason, or process anything. Things just stopped. There was nothing in my mind."

Monique's father picked her up and took her to Nancy, France. The funeral would take place in a few days, and Mr. Mayor would conduct the service for his friend's son and his would-be son-in-law. About 2,000 people were at the service. All of it seemed surreal as if it wasn't happening. Lucien went up to the front to speak. Monique remembered hearing her father's voice crack when he spoke about Pierre. This was hard for everyone, and Lucien was no exception. He struggled to watch his daughter go through this difficult time. When people came to shake her hand, Monique just went through the motions, unattached to what was swirling around her. Pierre's family was a well-known and respected family in Nancy. Many people came to the service, but Monique doesn't remember much about it. All she remembered was that she was in a state of shock for quite a while after the funeral.

Then the cards came. Most of them had the familiar Romans 8:28 in them: "And we know that in all things God works for the good of those who love him." Monique wondered what the good was in losing her fiancé.

After the funeral, Monique went back to Geneva to pack things up. She had no direction, plan, or purpose. Many people advised her to get away, but she didn't know what she wanted to do. The only thing that brought any kind of comfort to her was music. Her 20-year-old mind could not wrap itself around the idea of life and what it was supposed to mean.

"I knew God, but at the time life stung too much to call out to him," Monique shared. "I didn't know what steps to take next. I felt so shocked and numb to even question God or anything else for that matter. What was I to do now? I thought that getting married, having children, and doing life with Pierre was what my purpose was. Now I had nothing. I had not planned any farther than that. I was simply 20 years old."

Aunt Rosalie was Monique's favorite aunt, and her daughter Margarite was Monique's favorite cousin. The girls were like sisters. Shortly after the funeral, Aunt Rosalie invited Monique to come and stay with them for a while. Because Monique's parents were heading to the mission field, they had no home where Monique could stay. Margarite's sister, Doris, worked for a dentist in Basel, Switzerland, and was able to get Monique a job at the dentist's office.

Healing was exactly what Monique needed at that time, and it helped that she and her cousin were like very close sisters. They enjoyed life as best as they could. Visiting Margarite's boyfriend, Erich, while he was on leave from the military provided a great time for the three of them. It provided a much-needed distraction from the painful events of the past. Eventually, Margarite and Erich would marry. Monique was very happy for her cousin, but she still did not feel settled.

While Monique was in Basel, her family encouraged her to think about an au pair program conveniently located in Zurich. The company helped young European women get jobs as au pairs in America. It sounded promising to Monique. Her parents' lives had shifted in a new direction as well. They had not gone to Brazil after all but stayed in Nancy to start a church. During the summers, the Mayors also worked at the Credo in Wilderswil, Switzerland, helping at camps for young people. Her parents seemed settled, and now Monique could set out on a new path if it worked for her to go to America.

With her parents' support, Monique signed up with an au pair agency. When a young woman signed up with the au pair company, her name went on a list, and when there was a family in the United States who wanted an au pair, the young woman was expected to be packed and ready to go. Monique received her call to go, and in September 1952, she arrived in New York. It was one year after she and Pierre would have been married. Monique still felt numb and not excited about life, but she just took each day as it came. She was going through the motions of life and functioning as best she could, but that was it. Her faith was just another part of her life. She had learned to put one foot in front of the other and keep going.

Monique told me, "I had never been to the States and didn't know what to expect. I still was numb. I said goodbye to my family and boarded the ship. I was leaving war-torn Europe to sail to my new future. Here I was, the shy French girl leaving my past and pain behind me. I didn't want to look back, and yet I didn't know what lay ahead. I just simply went through the motions."

Monique's life was again about to change. Her experiences as a child, adolescent, and young adult were more things to put into her suitcase of life as she kept going. Monique told me that each experience helped prepare her to have the necessary tools for future situations. But now at 21 years old, she did not know how those experiences would help. At this point, she was glad to be leaving Europe and all the pain associated with her past.

CHAPTER FOURTEEN

Even the Poor Bear His Image

Widow's Might always checked on the widows they were helping, so Monique and I went to a village outside of Jinja. We drove down rutted roads where it seemed like we wouldn't be able to maneuver the car too much farther. We were going to a village where Widow's Might was helping a group of widows. As we drove up to a location that seemed difficult for even Google Earth to locate, the women rushed out to greet us. There was a typical mud hut that you picture when you think of Africa. Literally made of mud, the home had four walls with a door framed with wood. A couple of small windows were carved out of the mud to let in a little light. It had a thatched roof made of grasses and reeds that grew on the land. It felt like I was in the jungles of Africa.

The women had a few chairs set up for us so the Widow's Might workers could take care of the business side of things. The ministry had given them money to start a business of raising pigs.

They had done quite well with this program. As the pigs grew, they sold some of them so they had money to send their children to school. They also had two cows that they were very proud of. If people own cows, they are considered very wealthy. If the women had any questions about how to care for the livestock, they asked one of the ministry workers who visited them once a month. The worker would give them advice on what to do. They would also talk about the business side of things and get advice on how to keep their businesses going.

After we took care of business, we spoke some encouraging words to these women from Scripture. We then prayed with them, and they took us around to see all their livestock and crops. While we were visiting and encouraging them, they were preparing a typical meal for us. Pots were being used to cook the various types of food. The small charcoal fire was burning outside the hut, while another small charcoal fire was being used inside the hut. Once the food was ready, they invited us in to eat a meal with them. They ushered us into a small room that had about four chairs and a small table. We realized that there wasn't room for any of the widows, and we ended up eating by ourselves while the widows stayed outside. We ate Matoke bananas which were very delicious, a type of rice, some sauce, and some chicken. The meal was very tasty and filling.

As we got up to thank them and eventually leave, some of the younger children came around. Because the special guests had come, the children were taught not to bother us. They had stayed at a distance until they were allowed to come and meet us. They were very poor looking, but they didn't seem to know it, and it did not bother them. These children and women were human beings made in the image of God. They lived in mud huts, slept on woven mats on the ground with spiders and who knows what else crawling around, ate the food that grew around them, and worked to provide a life for themselves and their children. It was hard to wrap my thoughts around it and make any sense of it. Why is it that some humans live better than others? We all bear the image of God. Could we who live better reach out and help those who don't know they can live healthier, better lives? Is that not what God's love compels us to do—to help others in their distress? Do we not ask God to help us bring a bit of heaven to earth?

CHAPTER FIFTEEN

A New Life

We drove back to Jinja and closed up the office for the day. It was time for more stories about Monique's life that would last into the night.

Monique boarded the ship to begin her new life in America. The trip took five long days to get from France to New Jersey. Part of that excitement waned as the ship rocked on the Atlantic, but she had the urge to move forward. Once she landed in New Jersey, the company got her working as a nanny, or au pair, for a German woman. She ended up doing much more than what was in the contract. But Monique didn't say anything and continued working hard for this family.

She began taking English classes at night while maintaining her job during the day. She ended up working for the family from September 1952 through July 1953. The job was very difficult. The church Monique was attending found out how this family was treating her. They had to get a lawyer to get her out of the situation with this family. She was able to leave and began looking through the newspaper for another job. She found one working as an accountant in a carpet store for an Armenian man.

While Monique was adjusting to the States, she heard of a French club where people from France got together every so often to work on their English and comfort each other with French customs and foods.

"I decided to go," Monique said, "and once I was there, I began to make friends. One of the friends I met was an older French woman, Marie, and her family. She had a son named Michel."

The French people got together to celebrate Bastille Day on July 14, 1953. Marie invited Monique to her place where she was living with her daughter, her son-in-law, and Michel.

"Marie was quite ill with diabetes," Monique told me. "Her family took care of their mother because she was blind and knew no English. She was a lovely person. Her husband had passed away years ago when her daughter was around the age of four and her son was only three months old. They lived in France until Michel happened to come to America around 1947. Shortly after he came, his sister, her husband, and Marie followed.

"I worked constantly and returned to my rented attic room and fell asleep. I had made some friends from the church I attended who would invite me to their home for a meal after church on Sundays. There was a nice, older couple who picked me up and then dropped me back home on Sundays. Michel and his mother were my secular friends. Michel asked me to go on a date, and I immediately asked him to come to church with me. And he did. Soon Michel and I had gone out on a couple of dates.

"I wrote to my father about Michel and how I thought I was falling in love. He said I was to come home right then with all my belongings. In October 1953, I boarded a ship and immediately left for France. When I got home, my dad said that if Michel loved me, he would have to come and get me. As I look back, I believe my father saw that maybe I was in the relationship because I was rebounding from Pierre's death. My father was concerned and wanted to talk to Michel and see who he really was as a person.

"I also visited with Pierre's mother when I returned to France, and she talked to me because she also felt I was rebounding from Pierre's death. Even with my father's wisdom and Pierre's mother's insight, I felt I couldn't say no to Michel. I was afraid to give my own opinion or change my mind. I wasn't used to standing up for what I thought was important. I prayed that God would give me an answer. I thought that if Michel came, that would be my answer. I think back now and see that I was too inexperienced and was not used to thinking on my own and making my own decisions.

"I began thinking that maybe Michel wouldn't come. But then I heard from him, and he was on his way. His family encouraged him to go to France and marry me. Once in France, Michel told me what his mother had told him about coming to marry me, so I thought that was my answer. There was no formal engagement or even a ring. First, my father wanted to talk with Michel.

"It was now the first week of December, and my father took Michel aside and began to inquire about his relationship with Christ. Michel told my dad that he believed in Christ, and my dad took that as the answer he was looking for. After more conversations between Michel and my dad, I think my dad felt we did love each other, so he gave his blessing for us to marry.

"There was a lot of excitement because we were to be married soon. All the preparations went into high gear as we all worked to put this wedding in place. We were to be married on December 28, 1953, and my cousin Margarite helped with many of the wedding preparations. Being married in the same church she had gotten married in near Basel, Switzerland, where her father was the pastor, made getting into a church easy in a short period of time. I borrowed a dress, and the wedding took place.

"Since Michel had family in the south of France, we decided to travel throughout the area and visit with family for our honeymoon. This trip was the first time I realized how naïve I was and how Michel was much more experienced in the ways of the world. After a quick honeymoon by train through the south of France, we headed back to the States to begin our married life together in New Jersey."

CHAPTER SIXTEEN

Entering Rwanda: Youth Might

M onique had several meetings scheduled for the ministry in Rwanda, so she asked me if I would like to drive to another country and see what the ministry was doing over there. I was more than willing. We woke up early to head to Rwanda, the Land of a Thousand Hills. We packed up the Toyota with many supplies for the ministry. There was barely enough space for one more passenger and a backpack, but we got it done.

After driving into Kampala, we stopped and picked up one of Monique's dear friends. Ryan was a photojournalist who had connected with Monique and then helped out in various ways. Ryan and Monique shared the driving over very rough roads and potholes that swallow small cars if you are not alert enough to avoid them. After about six hours of driving and halfway there, we stopped in the Ugandan town of Mbarara at a restaurant Monique was familiar with. We unfolded our tired bodies from the car and used the restrooms. We then enjoyed lunch and had something to drink. Everything took over an hour to be served, but it was worth the break in the journey. After a decent meal and filling up the car with gas, we headed on to Rwanda. Monique knew the roads and towns very well and knew where and when to stop. There were very few places you could trust to use the facilities on such a long trip.

We finally arrived at the Rwanda border. It was a small village, and there were a few government offices on each side of the gate that separated the two countries. We had to stop and park the car on the Ugandan side and show our passports and vehicle papers. The border guards all knew Monique and greeted her pleasantly. Before we crossed over, Monique also had to stop in and check with the police. About 30 minutes later, we were free to cross the border, only to stop and do the same routine with the Rwandan officials. As we walked to the window to have our passports checked, they stamped our pages and issued our visas. The entire experience seemed a little surreal, but the workers looked very official and took their jobs very seriously, all the while working at their own relaxed pace.

The contrast between border checks or ports of entry I had been through, varied greatly. I was reminded that the border checks we just passed through were different, and different was okay. We were finally finished with all the paperwork and were free to continue on our journey.

My first thought on seeing Rwanda was how beautiful the landscape was. It was not what you usually think about African countries. We began driving on a winding road that took us into a forest. The hills were all terraced and lush with all kinds of vegetation. As we drove higher on the road, we could see down into a valley that looked like somewhere in Hawaii. Terraced hills reached up on the sides, and down in the valley cattle were roaming. The green valleys and the rich, red soil reminded me of what it might look like if Hawaii and England were combined and became a country.

As dusk came, the sun cast beautiful colors throughout the hills and valleys. Fog began to set in and covered the land with a blanket of mist. As we turned corners on the road, the valley opened up beyond us, and we could see quite a distance over more hills, gentle slopes, and fertile valleys.

The car continued its climb through the hills, and we eventually wound up in Kigali, the capital of Rwanda. It was late when we arrived at the home of the ministry of Widow's Might and Youth Might. We met up with a staff member who took Ryan and me to a guesthouse while Monique stayed in her room in the office. We had made it to Rwanda.

The guesthouse was very simple. The entry had a small wooden table where a woman sat with a notebook and registered our names and checked us in. We were given our keys and shown our rooms.

As I locked the door behind me and assessed my surroundings, I was reminded of a question Monique had asked me earlier. "Was I scared to go to Rwanda?" I could understand why she asked me that, given the conflicts there. Typically, I am not a fearful person, so I responded to her with a confident no. I love adventure and travel, and I had not come across anything in my travels so far that had made me afraid. But this guesthouse gave me an unsure feeling. I went back and unlocked the door to peek out and see how far down the hall Ryan's room was, just for reassurance to know that there was someone here I could trust.

I locked myself back in my room and prepared to go to bed. The window didn't close all the way, and there were guards right outside talking all night. Of course, I couldn't understand what they were saying. I do know they were carrying guns, and that felt a little intimidating. As I climbed into bed, I noticed there was no mosquito net to protect me from any malaria-carrying mosquitoes, and the curtains on the window did not close completely. But aside from these uncomfortable physical elements, I just did not feel at peace. I went to bed with my earbuds in and my iPod running all night.

Halfway through my somewhat sleep, I needed to use the bathroom. I quietly went into the bathroom but didn't turn the light on for fear of bringing unwanted attention to myself in the form of mosquitoes or guards. I could still hear the guards right outside my window, which I suppose should have provided some comfort, but I only felt vulnerable. The noises of the night were louder and different than what I was used to, which caused me to feel a bit on edge. I wandered back to my bed amid the blaring music coming from somewhere down the street, and I eventually got some sleep, as fretful as it was.

The next day seemed to correct all my wrong first impressions that had clashed with the beautiful scenery when I first entered this interesting country. Coming into a new place in the dark is never a fair assessment of any place. I realized how stories in the media could color our understanding of other cultures. There were no grounds for my fears as I enjoyed my time in that country. Had I developed preconceived beliefs about the Rwandan people before I had gotten to know them? That thought stopped me in my thinking and made me want to become aware of people's lives for who they are now, not keeping them in a place where others' views or stories direct the thoughts and attitudes we have of a people group. There was a great relief on my part after I thought things through with a lens of truth and accuracy. I found it somewhat maddening to think that a one-time incident in Rwandan history could color the ideas and fears about their culture still today.

After that first restless night in Rwanda, Ryan and I walked over to the ministry house and met up with Monique. She was already up and taking care of business. She was talking very seriously to a young man and setting things straight. Later we were told that he had lied about something, and she had heard about it. She was talking to him to find the truth about the situation. He was telling her how he was sorry, but Monique was getting ready to walk him over to the person he had wronged and insist that he make amends right then and there. She had to train these young people in things their parents should have taught them. These were the young people I was about to meet who had little chance in life or training for that matter.

These were the ignored orphans, as Monique called them—misfits in the sense that they didn't have a place to fit in or people to go to. They had lost their families during the Rwandan conflict in 1994 and had grown up without a family's nurturing. They also had missed out on an education. Many had the equivalent of a third to fifth-grade education and were now trying to make it in the grown-up world. As their stories were revealed to me when I met them, a spot in my heart softened. I was about to learn things that would forever change my heart and the trajectory of my energies and resources.

We walked around the house where the ministry and its workshops were. It was still quite early, and they were finishing their breakfast. At this point in the ministry's history, there were about 70 young people. Three of them were cooking a sorghum meal in a large pot over an open fire. It is similar to oatmeal and very healthy. The consistency was closer to a very thick drink. The workers gathered around with their cups and ate their breakfast before getting to work. If they did not have this breakfast, they would go without food for the day.

We continued to walk around and came upon an old torn military tent set up in the yard. The ministry had purchased wood for a woodcarving workshop where they made sculptures. When a sculptured piece sold, the worker got paid. These young adults could not just show up at the ministry and get paid to be there. They knew they had to work to get paid.

There were 15 to 18 young men sitting on stumps of wood or the wood-chip-covered ground. They used machetes and small handmade tools to carve beautiful pieces of art sculptures. I asked one of the English-speaking young men if I could take their picture while they worked. He interpreted to the working guys and explained to them what I wanted to do. They looked up shyly at each other and continued to work. I was standing near one young man with my camera when he picked up a machete and started swinging at a clump of wood. Whoa! It startled me, and I backed up with a bit of shock on my face.

He was very accurate as he delivered each strike to the wood. The chips flew while a figure slowly began to emerge. The work environment was far from optimal, and yet these young men produced very beautiful art. Each piece they carved was from one piece of wood with delicate and exact markings.

As I looked around at them, I noticed that some of them had scars on their heads, arms, and faces. They looked like they had been very deep, serious injuries at one time. It made me realize that time can heal much, but scars were a permanent part of their lives. It had affected their lives forever.

As I watched them work, they looked somewhat intimidating as they held those tools and whacked away at the wood. The tools were being used to create art and beauty for someone to enjoy. That is just like our God to take something that Satan intends for evil and use it for good. I smiled as I got ready to walk to another part of the ministry.

In another room in the house, about 12 people were gathered. They were sewing on treadle sewing machines making bags, kitchen hot-pad sets, aprons, and many other items. They smiled politely and kept working. Some of them were humming. Many of them seemed to be quite young. I would learn later that many of the girls who looked like they were 12 were actually 18 to 22 years old. Without the ministry of Youth Might, they would have been on the streets or involved in bad situations.

There are very few options available to young adults who have no family and no education, and yet the world looks at them as adults who should be making it on their own. The ministry had hired a widow who was very talented as a seamstress to teach these young adults the skills they needed to make sewn items. They knew they would get paid when their items sold. As I walked around the room to see what they were working on, some of their eyes seemed empty or hollow. Others seemed to know that they were now safe and that their dignity had been restored.

I continued down the hall to the living room. Several long tables were set up, and young people were working diligently on greeting cards. The designs on the cards were made from banana bark. They meticulously stripped small strands of the fiber from the bark and used them as lines to create pictures of all kinds on the front of cards. Beautiful pictures emerged as I watched them work quietly at the tables. Using a razor blade, homemade glue, and their fingers, they produced a unique form of art.

Before any of the workshops began each day, all the workers met and had a time of Bible study and prayer together. They now had a hope and a future after all hope had seemed to be dashed and destroyed before their very eyes.

2015 - Going back to the apartment Monique, her brother, and her father lived in together in Lausanne in 1944.

1951 - The books Monique had in Bible school later assisted her in starting her ministry to widows in New Jersey.

2018 - Distributing uniforms the workshops of the ministry sews so impoverished children can attend school in Rwanda.

2015 - The home Monique lived in as a child that was bombed during WWII.

2016 - Many of the young adults Monique ministered to were getting married. The weddings would consist of several couples getting married at the same time.

2018 - Monique handing out certificates to the workers involved with the ministry, helping the workers realize their value and worth.

CHAPTER SEVENTEEN

Married Life

Monique continued to tell me more of her story. After the trip through southern France with her new husband, the newlyweds headed back to the States to resume the jobs they had before they left for Europe. Once back in New Jersey, they set up their home, a furnished, rented room in someone's house. They both had jobs, cared for Michel's mother who lived with his sister and went about every day normally as anyone would expect.

It wasn't long before the couple was able to purchase a house. It was a cluster of three little sections—the main house, an apartment, and a small cottage in the back. The place needed a lot of repairs, and the two worked long hours renovating all three units. Monique was pregnant during that time, but she lost the baby. She ended up miscarrying three times from 1955 to 1956. Once again, Monique had suffered loss, and once again she just moved on from the hurt as she was so used to doing. Eventually, they lived in the main house and rented out the apartment and the cottage.

Michel's mother, Marie, moved in with them in the main house. She was blind, and Monique ended up taking care of her. Monique didn't mind since she was raised with the sense that when someone needed help, you helped. It was an automatic response for Monique.

Monique was again pregnant. Her pregnancy was good this time, but the birth was not a normal one. The baby was face up, and Monique was in labor 27 hours before the baby girl was born. Her next pregnancy was also good, but the delivery was again long and difficult. After 33 hours of labor, a second daughter joined the family. Another difficult thing for Monique was seeing her husband's reaction right after she had given birth. He wanted a boy and was clearly disappointed in Monique for not giving him a son.

Eventually, Michel accepted the fact that this was his family. Occasionally, they visited Monique's family who was in Canada, the United States, and Europe. Monique's brother, Bernard, was living in Canada, and her sister was in the United States. Monique and Michel's daughters were able to meet their cousins in Switzerland and get to know their grandparents. Sometimes the girls went alone to visit their relatives in Switzerland.

In 1964, Monique got another dreaded phone call. This time it was about her father. Her parents had been working at the Credo Inn in Wilderswil, Switzerland, when her father went down to the basement to check on the boiler. As he was going down the stairs, his heart stopped. He was only 61 years old. Mrs. Mayor called to him and then went down after she heard a thud.

The family was called, and funeral arrangements were made. Monique headed to Switzerland for the service. All of Monique's siblings were also able to attend the church on a hill with its spires pointing to heaven. The service for this man, Monique's beloved father, was packed. In his short years on earth, he had had a huge impact on many people's lives. Several people shared that when he spoke of being a Christian, they wanted to receive Christ all over again. The family had counted at least 70 families who were in ministry because of Lucien Mayor. On his tombstone were the words that reflected his life: Sauvé pour Servir—Saved to Serve.

Once again, the pain of life was etched into Monique's heart. Not only was her father gone but her marriage was also struggling. Throughout their 18 years together, Monique and Michel's struggles intensified.

Monique quietly shared, "One summer after we had sent the girls off to Europe to visit my family, our marriage unraveled to the point it could not be put back together. In the end, he divorced me. It was 1971, and it was embarrassing and deeply painful. I didn't know how to navigate through this time in my life. I never told my mom. I never told anyone because I thought that it would be a terrible thing for the daughter of Lucien Mayor, an evangelist, to get a divorce."

Michel and Monique split up their possessions equally. Monique worked hard and bought his portion of the house so she and the girls could have some stability. She continued to work hard at three jobs to support them. Shame and guilt were the emotions she lived, breathed, and surrounded herself with. Because of the guilt she put on herself and felt from others, she began falling into depression. It seemed to her that being divorced was an unforgivable sin. She didn't see any hope and felt she had no support or even a voice to speak out about what was happening to her. She wasn't sure she would make it.

Seeking help from a counselor or pastor was not the standard practice at that time. Often women were blamed for ending a marriage, and on top of that, divorce carried a stigma of failure and shame. Monique was already feeling shame and rejection, so she did what she thought she should do. She just walked on.

"I quit going to church because I was so ashamed. At that time, the Christian community viewed a person going through a divorce as dirt and pushed them away or excommunicated them. They had no pity. They didn't even talk to you. I felt stained, cast out, and unredeemable, especially since I was a Sunday school teacher and had organized a children's orchestra to play hymns at church."

Even the pastor of her church rejected her. All the others didn't know how to deal with a divorcee. She even felt abandoned by God. "I was brought up to walk in the way of God because that is what I knew to do. When something bad happens in your life, you find yourself in a circumstance that is not part of God's way or following the straight line. The fault is yours. I was like a little kid—don't do this, don't do that. I was an obedient person, not rebellious by nature. Now this great big thing I knew was wrong was happening to me. It was happening, and I was in it. I was on another road, away from what I had known to do. Now I was alone. Where could I turn? That was depression settling in. You are taken by something, and you do not know what to do, and no one is there for you. And of course, God is not there because it is not his way. He doesn't want anything to do with anything that would go against him. This is what I was thinking at the time."

Monique found no support from the outside and no support emotionally, financially, or, of course, spiritually. Her siblings didn't even know that she had divorced, and two of them lived in North America. She was very alone and felt she had to rely only on herself. She realized she only had herself, she was to blame, and she had messed up.

In 1974, Monique met a guy at work. He seemed to accept Monique for who she was. But Monique didn't feel worthy of love because she was a divorced person. She continued feeling guilt-ridden and non-deserving of anything good, and she was exhausted. She continued to carry all the responsibilities and guilt of the divorce on herself. Revealing her secret to anyone was not an option, and the way she was brought up only compounded the pressure building up inside of her.

Life had become too much. Her three jobs required her to work at her regular job from 8:00 a.m. to 5:00 p.m., run home and see the kids, get to work at her second job by 6:00 p.m. and work until midnight, and then pick up shirts for ironing, which was her third job. Waves of guilt washed over her and kept her depressed and downcast, especially knowing the other mothers in the neighborhood were all stay-at-home moms. She began to drink to ease the pain, which didn't work. It only complicated the matter and increased her problems. Raising her daughters by herself and dealing with the typical teenage rebellion was a daily struggle. She was working three jobs to cover the expenses for all three of them. Feeling the rejection of many around her, she constantly carried the feelings of being a failure as a wife, a Christian, a mother, and the daughter of Lucien Mayor. All that became so heavy that she felt she couldn't take it anymore.

A downward spiral effect took over. The choices and decisions she made were directly opposite to everything she had been taught growing up and what she understood to be the right way to live. All these bad choices seemed natural and easy as if she wasn't in control of her life. She gravitated toward what she knew was wrong and painful. This force of evil seemed to take over, and she didn't know how to stop it. She didn't have any healthy support system when she needed it most. In 2 Corinthians 7: 9–10, Scripture talks about how grief can lead a person to salvation, but worldly grief or guilt leads to death. That latter type of grief was swallowing her whole.

Monique felt she had no place to turn, so she thought the only way to deal with all of this was to "get off the world" (Monique's words). It all came to a head one day. She came home from work, physically exhausted from lack of sleep, heavy guilt, and insurmountable pressures on all fronts. Even her relationships were falling apart. She felt she couldn't handle another moment. The shame and guilt she carried were just too much, and she decided to end it all.

It was late in the evening when a friend stopped by and found her. Her friend rushed Monique to the hospital. It was then that Monique began to wake up. Not only did she begin to wake up to life, but she began to wake up to many insights, truths, and realities.

The first reality that struck her with full force was the idea that she had to become a better person for her children. She had to. She had to find a way to push past the guilt and shame and move on. That was one thing she knew how to do. Maybe now this grief would move her to God and not away from him. The realization that she must be a better person for her children was the catalyst that urged her to take the first step toward healing.

She decided it was time to go to church so the girls had a place to go. She still didn't feel worthy of church, but her daughters surely were. Monique had a summer home on the coast, and she decided to attend church there. No one would know her there. She could make a new start. The first sermon she heard was from Psalm 103:11–12, "For as high as the heavens are above the earth, so great is his love for those who fear him; as far as the east is from the west, so far has he removed our transgressions from us."

Here was the great evangelist's daughter hearing this for the "first" time. It poured over her heart like refreshing rain. Monique wept. For the first time since her divorce, she felt liberated from all the guilt, shame, and lies. She could simply turn to God and allow him to carry her. She did not need to hold it together in her own strength.

This was the God she began to turn to, slowly at first. She was not turning to a set of rules or church doctrine but to God alone. She was in a desperate and vulnerable place, and she knew she needed a Savior. This was the beginning of her true redemption.

She marveled at how God had orchestrated the words the pastor read from Scripture, that God did love her beyond what she could imagine. After being in church all her life, she felt God would hate her after what she attempted to do. It was so refreshing to feel that God was speaking specifically to her in that church. It felt like God was waiting at the door to welcome her in.

Life was beginning to turn around for Monique. She felt safe in this church and even ran into some old friends. Another turning point for her was that she met other people who had gone through divorces. Sharing each other's stories helped Monique see more accurately that what she had gone through was not just her fault. Maybe she wasn't so stained as the enemy was out to make her feel. Healing was slowly happening, and Monique began to depend on others instead of feeling she had to have it all together on her own.

Two years after the divorce, Monique's mother found out. Nervous about what her mother would say, Monique began to tense up, expecting rejection and shame. But that is not what happened. Her mother did not reject her and instead seemed to understand the pain and hurt Monique had gone through. It seemed that just maybe Monique's darkest hours were over.

After Monique shared these stories with me, I could tell it had been very difficult for her to disclose this information. She was making herself vulnerable, but she now seemed to understand that there was a benefit to sharing some of these sins. As I began to think through her life story and pair it with history, I began to see that when awful, horrible tragedies take place, the victims still have a choice to either move toward God or away from God.

Many simply can't move toward God because the trauma is too great. The shame and guilt the enemy uses can destroy people. Somehow, Monique moved toward God—not religion and not the world—and was offered forgiveness and joy to carry on instead of losing hope, becoming bitter, and living an angry and lifeless existence.

Monique was now able to help others move toward God—toward hope and life—instead of desperation and death. She was well acquainted with those shadows in the valleys of death, yet she also knew she could raise her face to the Creator whose love is not condemning or reflective of what humans have devised as truth. It was with this knowledge that Monique was able to reach out and help others raise their faces to the Creator and know they were loved just as they are.

CHAPTER EIGHTEEN

Philippe

Before Monique came to Rwanda, there was an organization there that worked with street kids. The center physically cared for street kids, but there was no spiritual input. A woman at the center asked if Monique would come and help with some spiritual training. When Monique came to spiritually encourage these street kids, many of them connected with her.

The center would take care of kids up to the age of 18, and then they had to leave and live on their own. Many of them returned to living on the streets. They had no family and no job skills, so the streets were the only way of life they were familiar with.

Monique felt she needed to do more for these kids than just preach to them. She was also aware of the need for a safe house for these kids to transition from the care center to living on their own. She knew of a guesthouse in town that could possibly work to house these young adults. Monique saw to it that the guesthouse was purchased and would be used as an interim time for young adults to learn a skill, eventually find work, and keep them from returning to the streets.

It was 1998 when Philippe met with Monique. She had a meeting in Kigali, Rwanda, where 500–600 young people came. There she spoke about Christ and shared His love for each of the young people. Sitting in the front row was a street kid named Philippe who had lived in the dumps for 11 years. As Monique shared about receiving Christ, Philippe raised his hand. He wanted to know more about Christ and his love.

Monique followed up with Philippe and met with him to encourage him in his new faith. At the age of 18, Philippe was going to secondary school (high school). He worked hard to support himself so he could continue his schooling. During his breaks from school, Monique asked him to help at the ministry house in Kigali. They were little jobs, but Philippe trusted Monique and enjoyed being around the ministry. Monique wanted to know how Philippe was doing in school and went to visit the school director. The report was that he was doing well. However, there were always problems with school fees. Monique knew people in Switzerland who were willing to help with school fees for street kids. Between Monique and the people in Switzerland, Philippe was able to continue his education.

Now Philippe was able to live at a secondary boarding school to finish his education. Whenever school was on break, he came to visit Monique. She often took Philippe and other former street kids to a restaurant, and many times it was the first time they had ever been to one. When she asked if they had had enough to eat or if they wanted more, they always looked around sheepishly and asked for more.

After Philippe finished school, he worked for Monique in small ways. First, it was helping with workshops and then with packing handcrafted items to be shipped. He was always efficient and helpful. God had changed his life through the instrument of Monique. She remembered Philippe as a former street kid who now had hope and a future because people were there to be the hands and feet of God. Philippe embraced the love of God by responding favorably to Monique and others who reached out to help just a simple street kid. In turn, Philippe was helping others know of God's love by reaching out and helping in ways he could.

As Monique told me the story of Philippe, she reflected on her journey and how her experiences had prepared her to meet people like Philippe. She shared how her experiences helped pack her suitcase so she would be prepared when she met people like Philippe. Sharing the difficult parts of her story seemed to validate what she did to endure, allowing hope to rise out of difficult life experiences.

CHAPTER NINETEEN

Hopeful for a New and Better Chapter

After her divorce, Monique began attending a new church. She continued working hard to pay the bills and raise her daughters. She began to allow herself to get to know a gentleman she had met at work.

"I met a charming man at work," she said. "I went in very early and worked as the accountant. The company was large and had several departments. The gentleman was from a different department than where I worked. We met at the coffee machine before most of the other workers came in. We started chatting one morning and found out we were both readers. We talked about what books we had read and what we found interesting about the books. We became friends over coffee and books. He seemed very kind and tenderhearted. We started bowling with the company team."

Monique lit up as she started telling me about Luke, the man at work. He was affectionate and treated Monique with value.

He served her. It was the first time she truly felt and understood the kind of love two people can share. Eventually, they decided to marry.

September 1975 was when Monique genuinely began to enjoy life. "I truly felt that God had given me a gift," she said. "Luke treated me kindly in so many ways. After many years of life being a struggle, I felt that God was giving me a glimpse of His goodness. Luke and I enjoyed life. That seemed to be a first for me in a long time. It was such a breath of fresh air. Being married to him was a joy."

As Monique's daughters grew up, went to college, and eventually got married, Luke and Monique found they had time to travel. Monique was able to quit work, and they went on road trips. Traveling extensively throughout the United States, Europe, and much of Canada provided good times for both of them. Life was like wave after wave of blessing and goodness for Luke and Monique.

They continued to live on the New Jersey coast and had a home that looked out on the bay. Monique remembered the little things Luke did to demonstrate his love for her. In the winter, as she was getting ready for bed, he would lie on her side of the bed so it would be warm for her when she climbed in. It was always those little thoughtful things that warmed her heart and soul.

This season of her life was such a contrast to the time before she was married to Luke. Monique became a grandmother, enjoyed life with her daughters, was active in her church, and enjoyed being loved and married. Her life was full and blessed.

* * * * *

By 1982, Monique was getting used to the goodness of life. Sure, there were normal struggles here and there, but overall, life couldn't have been better. Driving home one day with her daughter and granddaughter in the car, they passed by the parking lot entrance of an atomic plant. As they passed, a car came through the stop sign from the parking area and ran into the driver's side of Monique's car. When the ambulance came, Monique seemed to be okay. Her hand was swollen, but they were concerned about the other two passengers and attended to them first. Since Monique's daughter and granddaughter checked out, they turned their attention to Monique and walked her over to the ambulance. All three of them got into the ambulance, and while the nurse was asking questions, Monique felt like she was sinking into herself. When the next question came, all she could hear was a faraway staccato sound. The sinking feeling continued, but she didn't feel any pain.

At the hospital, the medical team took Monique's daughter and granddaughter back to treat one of them for a gash on the leg. Monique was still experiencing that sinking feeling. The team then took Monique back to examine her. While taking X-rays, they realized that Monique's neck was broken. This severe spinal injury between the second and third vertebrae can be fatal. By now her husband had arrived, and Monique heard the doctor talking to him. She heard Luke gasp. Suddenly about 12 medical staff personnel were surrounding her and putting sandbag-type things around her to stabilize her movements. They put four screws in her skull so they could attach a weight system that would slowly pull the spinal column back into place. She was put in a Stryker frame to stabilize her neck so she could heal. A Stryker frame is placed around a patient so they can be turned over without moving.

For Christmas in 1981, about a year before, Monique's mother had given her a book called *Joni: An Unforgettable Story*. It is a story of a young woman who became completely paralyzed from the neck down from a diving accident when she was 17 years old. A friend of the family had translated the book into French, and Monique's mother thought it would make a great gift for Monique.

She had read the book and thought how sad it was that this young woman's life was so impacted by a simple accident. She had also thought how terrible it would be if her daughters ever had to go through something like that.

In April 1982, just four short months after she read Joni Eareckson Tada's book, she would be in the same type of Stryker frame. Here she was in that frame, but she was so thankful she wasn't paralyzed. Here is where Monique could see that Romans 8:28 seemed to work for her. She would be able to walk again. Because she had read that book just four months ago, she felt God had given her that information to help her understand her situation. Monique knew she would walk again, so she turned her pain and frustration into gratitude and continued to heal.

Including therapy, Monique was in the hospital for two years and had many surgeries so she could heal completely. She was in a wheelchair for another year after she was released from the hospital. She still couldn't walk on her own, and she was very weak. Once she was out of the hospital, she was told that she needed another surgery. That felt like the straw that broke the camel's back. How could she go through another surgery? She cried out to God but was ready to push on or just take that next step—one foot in front of the other. When Luke and Monique were in the consultation meeting for another surgery, the X-ray revealed that the place that needed surgery had healed on its own. Just when Monique thought she couldn't take it anymore, God healed that part of her body. Maybe now her life would return to normal.

Luke was instrumental in helping her heal. He became her support, assistant, mobilizer, and joy. Going out of his way on the way to work, he would go to the hospital to lift her spirits. The nurses would flip Monique in her Stryker frame so she would be face up. Luke would give her a morning kiss and then take off for work. Constantly bringing laughter and encouragement, he was instrumental in her healing process.

Few people think of the side effects of things like major car accidents. After Monique was able to live at home, she developed agoraphobia, a fear of open spaces. Because she was in the Stryker frame for so long, any spacious areas seemed to shut her down. One time as she went to the mailbox to get the mail, she felt an overwhelming paralysis. She couldn't move and had to sit down on the driveway. She remembered another time when she and Luke went to the mall. Luke had to hold her hand and help her take one step at a time. From then on, he always held her hand in any open areas.

Healing was a long, slow process, but Monique could see that she was healing. Even through all the difficulties, she pressed on. Her body was getting stronger, and she was beginning to feel that life would return to normal in a very short time.

CHAPTER TWENTY

Renewed Hope

One aspect of Monique's ministry, whether in Uganda or Rwanda, was helping orphans attend school. There was one particular orphan the ministry helped start primary school. The student worked hard and did well throughout the primary school years. Then it was time to advance to secondary school. Because the young man worked hard and had good grades, the ministry supported him in secondary school. Throughout his years there, he did well and kept his grades high. While he attended secondary school, he worked any type of job during school breaks. He was a conscientious, hard worker.

Once he finished secondary school, he wanted to go to the university. However, the ministry did not offer to pay for the university. He had the grades and the motivation, but he did not have a scholarship or a sponsor. He finally came to Monique and asked if she could help him. Those were the kind of questions that broke Monique's heart. How do you turn a young man away from his aspirations?

Monique came up with a plan. She shared with the young man that he should get a job and work during the week, which would allow him to take classes on weekends. That would work, but it would take longer than normal for him to finish at the university. The young man decided to take Monique's advice and did as she suggested.

He soon had a job and signed up for weekend classes. He worked hard. While he was in school, he saved every bit of money he could. Paying for his education brought him much satisfaction. Finally, he finished school and got a good job. He had some land and built a house. Later, he met a girl, and soon they were married.

During a visit from a ministry director, the young man wanted to share his story. He told how he was blessed to go to school because of Monique. It had changed his life for the better. The idea of helping someone through school had such an impact on him that he is now helping others go to school. That is what the ministry is about—helping them help themselves. And now this young man is helping others.

Not all stories turn out this way, but many young adults were affected by the ministry and are now helping others. Monique prayed that what happened to this young man would happen to many others she helped. When young adults are given hope because someone takes the time to give them some dignity, great things can happen. That is the beauty of taking what you have and reaching out to others.

CHAPTER TWENTY-ONE

Another Valley of Death

Ever since Monique's husband, Luke, was 20 years old, he had had ulcers. Having pain in his abdomen was nothing new for him. But now there was a pain that was extremely intense and different than what he had experienced before.

While Monique was still in rehab, Luke decided to go to the doctor to have his pain checked out. Monique decided to call the doctor and talk to him about Luke's test results. When she heard the news, she asked the director of the rehab center if she could go home for the weekend.

When Luke came to visit, he found Monique ready to go home for the weekend. Of course, Luke was delighted to have her home for a few days, but Monique couldn't bring herself to tell Luke the bad news the doctor had already told her about his test results. They enjoyed the weekend as much as they could, and on Sunday they headed to church. It was good to be sitting in church, even in a neck brace. The weight of telling Luke the test results was weighing heavily on Monique, but she knew that when you love someone, you face the good and the bad together. At the end of the service, the choir sang "I Surrender All." The song seemed to have an interesting way of showing up in very challenging times.

They went home, and Monique shared with Luke that the pain he was feeling was cancer—colon cancer. Luke took the news much better than Monique thought he would. He said, "Some people have heart attacks, some people die in car accidents, and I have cancer. Don't worry." Throughout Monique's life, she had learned that you take whatever news it is, do what you can with it, and move in a forward direction.

After consulting with the doctor, Luke was advised to have surgery. It was now December 1984. The doctors removed most of the cancerous colon, but Luke would need chemotherapy.

Monique was ready to be released from the hospital, even though she still had difficulty walking. Now it was her turn to care for Luke as he had cared for her. She worked at getting stronger, knowing that Luke would need her to help him physically.

By March 1985, Luke needed more surgery. As the doctors went in to remove more of his colon, they found that the cancer had gone into his bones. He was given three months to live.

Monique was used to difficulties, and every time life's evils and hardships struck, she had learned to walk on again. When the news came that Luke had little time left to live, they both released their tears and frustrations. But overall, Monique knew she had to "walk on." She realized later that doing that was not always healthy. Life seemed to be made up of some "goods" and a lot of "bads." She had learned long ago to face them all, do what she could at the moment, and walk on.

Luke had an incredibly courageous and positive outlook on the situation. He told Monique that he wanted to go to Switzerland for three weeks. He had come to love the place Monique was from, so they packed their bags and headed off to visit family, friends, and the wonders of Switzerland.

While traveling around Switzerland, they were able to see friends, stay with family, and generally enjoy their time. Luke was beginning to weaken. The pain was still there, but he pushed through it. Monique knew it wasn't easy, but she also knew he didn't want to give in and allow the pain to take over his love for life and Switzerland.

After three weeks, they headed back to New Jersey. The doctors had confirmed that the pain was there for a reason. The cancer was growing. Another surgery was necessary. Once they opened Luke up, the medical staff realized that the surgery would not be successful. The cancer was raging throughout his entire body. They did what they could, removed more of the cancer, closed him back up, and told him to make himself as comfortable as possible.

He had an amazing outlook on life. Monique brought him home and ministered to his ailing body. They enjoyed the time they had together even though it was much different than the first years of their marriage. They celebrated their 10th wedding anniversary amid Luke's pain. He was losing weight and was in a lot of pain, but he still smiled just because Monique was by his side. It was getting near the end of his life. Christmas was near, and it had been a year since he had been diagnosed with cancer.

On January 20, 1986, at 7:00 in the evening, Luke called out Monique's name. Throughout that night, Monique stayed by his side and played some hymns that Luke had sung in a barbershop chorus. Throughout the night, Luke seemed calm as if God were saying that He was ready to receive Luke into his arms. At 4:31 a.m. on January 21, Luke breathed his last breath. This 6-foot, 190-pound man's body was now 70 pounds, ravaged by the cruel and ugly disease of cancer, and yet he still smiled. The journey was over for Luke. He was finally rid of the pain that took over his body. For Monique, there was a gentle release of the burden of watching her loved one endure pain. There was also the great emptiness that engulfed her heart, soul, and mind. Her Luke who had showed her what love and laughter were, the man who brought joy to her life, was gone.

God had given Monique a beautiful gift through Luke. After going through the worst part of her life when she thought life wasn't worth living, Luke was there. Now he was gone. Once again, Monique knew she needed to walk on in the power of God's love. She needed to pull from His love and strength to take the next step in life.

Again, well-intentioned friends gave her Romans 8:28. She remembered telling God that she hated this verse because she could not see any good in losing her Luke. What good could come from death? There was no sense in trying to reason when a person is in the midst of such loss and pain. Every time Monique experienced loss, it seemed as if another heavy brick was added to her suitcase, and it was getting very difficult to carry. Once again, Monique tried to rise up and take the necessary steps to walk on.

CHAPTER TWENTY-TWO

Hope Was Found

When Monique first met Francois, he was a street kid teaching art at the youth center directed by a Swiss woman. He was not only teaching art but was also a motorcycle taxi driver. Always a hard worker, Francois felt responsible to help a younger sibling attend school. Life was not easy, but Francois carried on as best he could.

During his time at the youth center, Francois attended the youth meetings Monique had for the street kids. It was during this time that he heard about God's love for him. Being a sincere, quiet, and responsible person, Francois decided to commit his life to God and get baptized. He was never the type to follow the crowd or do something just because everyone else was doing it. He sensed God's love for him and wanted to follow God. His decision to follow Christ led him to a better life.

With his earnings from his job, he was able to build a house in Kigali and help send his sibling to school. Not long after the house was built, the government had plans to build a road exactly where his house was. There was nothing he could do but accept the small amount the government paid him to leave his home. It was time to move elsewhere in hopes of a better life.

He decided that Uganda looked like a good option. He left Rwanda and moved there. He found a job delivering milk from his bicycle. His work ethic came into play, and he became successful. However, he did not like the part about starting work at 2:00 a.m. every day.

Monique was in touch with Francois' sibling and managed a time to reunite the two. When they met, Monique invited Francois back to Rwanda to work for Youth Might. She needed people who could package up artwork the youth were creating and send them to France. Francois had good business sense and was not willing to take just any offer, so after some negotiations on how much he would be paid, he accepted the job. He moved back to Rwanda and was glad to be back home.

Shortly after he moved back, Monique moved the ministry to another town. The move was in Francois' favor. He knew the culture and had connections to the people in that area. Moving with Monique to the new area was significant for the ministry as well since Francois knew the area and was able to help secure the workshop buildings and a place for Monique to live and have an office.

The ministry was growing, and Francois was a natural leader who could help the ministry in many ways. God had put Monique in his life, which had given him newfound hope. Due to his leadership abilities, good business sense, cultural awareness, strong work ethic, and honesty, he became a leader in the ministry and a great help to Monique. God met Francois when life was difficult. His hard work and love for God gave him hope for the future. His infectious smile and laughter were clear signs of the blessings he shared with others.

CHAPTER TWENTY-THREE

Widowhood

Widowhood—what a hollow-sounding word. It's a status no woman wants, never signs up for, and never looks forward to. It is placed or forced on her on some of her darkest days. That is exactly how Monique felt.

Monique had always felt that she had to be strong. She believed that if you are a Christian, you can't show weakness. Yet she was dying inside. There was so much pain and hurt inside of her, and yet she didn't think there was anything she could do about it. As she always said, you just walk on. Monique was no stranger to pain, yet each time she dealt with it face to face, she chose to push through and do what she could to move on.

Luke was buried on Friday, January 24, 1986. As Monique headed home for the first time without Luke and drove up the driveway, she realized she would now have to unlock the door, something he had always done. It was the first of many overwhelming incidents she would experience in widowhood.

Just two days later, Monique was back at church singing in the choir on Sunday. With a lump in her throat, mouthing the words as she sang and holding back tears, she pushed through the reentry into her new station in life. She was in survival mode, or better yet in her words, "the showing off mode." That came from her belief at that time that if you are a Christian, you know God is there as the God of all comfort, and therefore you *should* have the attitude that all is well.

Monique's situation led her to understand that other widows were experiencing the same types of things, and she sensed that they needed to be strong and push on so no one could judge their spirituality. That type of faulty thinking was harmful to these women, but at the time they didn't know any better.

One day in church, the congregation began singing a hymn. During the song, Monique noticed a woman who had recently lost her husband run out of the church. Monique followed the woman out of the church and put her arms around her. The woman told Monique that the hymn was her husband's favorite song and that it was just too much for her. She broke down in tears.

Then there was Aunt Mary, a family friend who had become like an aunt to Monique's children. She had been married to Frank for 51 years. On February 19, 1988, Frank died of Lou Gehrig's disease. At 7:00 a.m. on March 1, Mary called Monique who heard screaming on the other end. She recognized Mary's voice and immediately drove to her home. When she opened the door, Mary was crying and kept saying "the calendar, the calendar." Monique put her arms around Mary and asked her what it was about the calendar. Mary choked out, "He always did it."

Mary had come into the kitchen and noticed that the calendar needed to be switched to March. Her husband had always changed the calendar because he was the first one in the kitchen every morning. That was the first time Mary was faced with doing this small task. Imagine that for 51 years—612 times—Mary's husband had turned the calendar. After a person is widowed, it's the little things that sneak in and surprise them. Others who have not gone through this have a hard time understanding these experiences or feelings.

Seeing other widows experience loneliness and the deep pain inside, Monique felt it important that widows get together and support each other. Sensing that God had given her this thought, she felt she needed to bring others together to uplift, comfort, and encourage each other because she understood where they were coming from. Looking back at her own redemption, she knew the value of encouraging one another instead of trying to go through grief alone. She found that she and other widows were trying to put on a front and let the world know that all was well when it was not.

Romans 8:28 began to make sense. All the pain and suffering Monique had experienced was now working for good. Monique told me, "I went to my Sunday school superintendent and asked, 'Why don't we have a class for women in the church?' She responded, 'How can I have a class for them when I don't have enough teachers for the classes I already have?' I went home that day, and my eyes looked up at a bookshelf where I had many books. Way in the corner, God led my eyes to where I had placed my notebooks from my days at Bible school in Geneva some 28 years ago. I took one of the notebooks and began looking through it. I came across a section on the Psalms. It was training I had received years ago. It was as if God was telling me that I was the one who not only had the training but that he had prepared me years ago for this moment. This was not what I had in mind. Surely there was someone else to do it, and they would be much better and more capable to lead. The message from God was very precise that I was the one he was going to use to put his plan into action to encourage these women."

Monique decided to take some time to pray about this and see what she thought God was doing and if she was competent to take this on. In the quietness of her prayers and talking to God, she realized that God doesn't cast aside the things in our past. She began to put some puzzle pieces of her own life together and realized that she might be a person God could use to help others in their tough times.

Monique began to connect the dots of her life, including her childhood memories of World War II, her fiancé dying weeks before their wedding, her first marriage and how it ended so painfully in divorce, the loneliness and depression she experienced, the thief of cancer, and now her new title of widowhood. God had a purpose for her. She had learned to walk through the worst of situations, and God had been there every single time. The words from the book of Esther rang true: "For such a time as this" (Esther 4:14). Monique believed God had been there with her in every one of those experiences. There is a belief in God and then there is an assurance in God. She had the belief, and now she had the assurance. She decided to put one foot in front of the other. Needless to say, she began teaching the Sunday school class.

The church put an announcement in the bulletin that a women's class was now available. All women were welcome to attend. Monique was very shy and didn't like to speak in front of people. She remembered shaking inside during those early class sessions. But she was determined to share with these women. It was clear that they were very excited to be part of something like this.

Later, Monique began inviting widows to her home and started a group to support each other during that time of their lives. Widows came to her home just for a time to chat or share stories about their loved ones who had passed away. Healing began to take place as they learned how to function in their new stage of life. The group started with just eight women meeting on Friday evenings, and it eventually grew to 255 women coming from surrounding churches.

Sometimes women shared that they slept in a shirt that had belonged to their husband or that they couldn't open a drawer where some of his personal belongings were still kept. The women needed to know that they were okay, that grieving is different for everyone, and that they were not going crazy.

The ministry grew and was meeting a need. Now not only widows were coming; single women were attending as well. Whether they were never married, divorced, or widowed, Monique knew the women needed to support each other. This group of women called themselves WOTO—Women on Their Own. Monique's home became known as Widow's Haven.

A woman named Patricia (Pat) had moved and was attending the church where Monique had the Bible study for women. Pat's mother was living with her but was now ill and in the hospital. The church knew about the mother being in the hospital and asked Monique if she would visit her. While Monique was at the hospital with the mother, the hospital said she would be released by the weekend. Later, Monique called Pat to see how her mother was doing. Pat burst into tears. Monique asked if she was okay and wondered if they could meet for coffee. They worked it out to meet later that week. Before they hung up, Pat thanked Monique for visiting her mother and said she was very touched that someone would visit her. That was the beginning of another friendship.

Over coffee, Pat began to share her story. In a very hushed, shameful tone, she told Monique she was divorced and felt like everyone looked at her as if she wore the scarlet letter. Pat knew Monique was teaching a Bible study for women at the church. Looking her in the eye, Monique shared that she, too, had been divorced. Monique's words shocked Pat who then shared that she had been married to a very abusive man. What made it so hard was that they had been very involved in the church, and her husband had even been a leader. When Pat tried to reach out for help, she was told that if she left him, it would be her fault. After years of enduring the abuse, Pat decided enough was enough, especially when her husband tried to abuse their daughter. Pat secretly met with attorneys and counselors and finally had the strength to leave her husband. That was why she had recently moved to the area where she met Monique.

Pat's guilt and shame were the same guilt and shame Monique was so familiar with. Once again, Monique could see the meaning of Romans 8:28. Things were beginning to work together for good. She could now help others when they were going through similar life experiences.

Women on Their Own was growing, supplying the necessary encouragement to women. They had lunch together once a month and had weekly meetings for ongoing support. As Monique was helping others, she began to realize this was helping her to not feel sorry for herself. Helping others was cathartic, and yet there was still some amount of hurt and pain inside. Discouragement began to raise its ugly head. After three years of being widowed and reaching out to others, Monique felt tired. She realized later that she had never properly grieved Luke's death.

All the while, Pat and Monique were becoming good friends, and Monique was an encouraging friend to Pat. A few years later, Pat's brother saw the positive and encouraging effect Monique had on his sister and suggested that Pat go on vacation to Bermuda and take Monique with her. It was 1989, the same year Ferne Sanford had gone to Bermuda at the invitation of a friend. This retreat was something Monique needed, and she knew it. She gladly accepted, and Pat and Monique went off to Bermuda. Little did Monique know that a divinely appointed meeting was going to take place.

Women on Their Own had been going on for quite some time when Monique met Ferne. Both women had a heart to help others. At that point, neither knew how their future would involve the plan of God. Monique told me, "Over the years, I came to understand more deeply that God never has us experience things in vain. It seems that he permits all these experiences so he can carry out his plan at another place or time *if* we are willing to work alongside God when he chooses to act."

Romans 8:28 began to make sense now. Monique could see that even being divorced could work for good.

CHAPTER TWENTY-FOUR

The Might of Widows

Monique and Pat were now on their way to Bermuda for a much-needed break. During that same time, Ferne was working at Washington Bible College as a dorm mom, and a woman named Eleanor was the secretary to the school's president. Eleanor was single, and her aunt had recently died and left her some money. Because she and Ferne were friends, she took Ferne on a vacation—to the same resort in Bermuda where Monique was staying because of her gracious friend Pat.

Monique and Ferne ended up sitting at the same table, and they began to share about their lives and how they both were widows. Monique shared that she had started a support group using the pen pal idea to encourage other women. They began sharing their stories and found that they shared many of the same pains and heartaches. They also shared their desire to help others who had found themselves in similar situations.

Monique and Ferne bonded over many aspects of how God had worked in their lives and brought them together, even at that resort. It would be the beginning of a long, lasting friendship.

After they all left the resort, Monique and Ferne continued to in stay touch, and Monique invited Ferne to come to New Jersey. Ferne lived in Pennsylvania. During Ferne's visit, she told Monique about Africa. She and her husband had served there as missionaries, and she now had a desire to return. After her husband died, Ferne had served as a dorm mother at a missionary school, Rift Valley Academy in Kenya. Ferne wasn't sure what she would do in Africa if she went back.

Ferne still had connections with a group of missionary kids she had known from her days at Rift Valley Academy. In 1990 and 1991, she went to Jinja, Uganda, with a group of these students, serving as the cook for this short-term mission trip. She met the parents of one of the former students there, and Ferne shared her desire to return to Africa, not sure what she could do. The missionary couple encouraged her to use her life as a widow to help other widows in Uganda.

There were many widows in Uganda at the time due to Idi Amin's years of terror in the 1970s when his regime had killed so many men in the country. Later, in the 1980s, AIDS became an epidemic. Because polygamy was practiced in Uganda, many women were also infected with AIDS. In that culture, when a man died, the husband's family would take in the widow and her children to care for them and help raise the children. When the AIDS epidemic affected so many people in Uganda, many husbands' families blamed the wives for the infections and ultimately their sons' deaths. Rejected and disgraced, young widows and their children were left alone to fend for themselves. Women simply were not valued in that society.

Ferne knew that women were nothing without children and even less without a husband. They also had no way to support themselves and their children. For many women, it was a very harsh reality. Not only were many women widowed but many of them would die from AIDS, leaving their children orphaned.

Ferne returned from her short-term trip but then went back to Uganda to visit the couple who had encouraged her to help widows. Through the friendship with that couple, Ferne met a Ugandan widow who had been a pastor's wife. Through that connection, the pastor's wife talked about ways to encourage other widows in Uganda. That was the beginning of Ferne's ministry in Uganda.

A seed had been planted in Monique's heart on that vacation to the Bahamas. She wanted to create retreats for women at her home in New Jersey. She had the perfect place—a home on the beach, and she lived there alone.

In the meantime, Monique and Ferne stayed in contact and developed their friendship. Ferne came to New Jersey to visit Monique several times, and the women became very close friends. Ferne had been widowed longer than Monique and became a great comfort and encouragement to Monique. Monique decided to ask Ferne to come and speak to her WOTO ministry to encourage the women like she had been encouraged. Monique's friendship with Ferne would be the foundation for the next chapter in Monique's life.

In 1991, Ferne started a pen pal ministry in Uganda to minister to widows there. She set out for Africa alone. Monique and Ferne continued to correspond with each other as they worked with their different ministries. Monique was continuing her ministry to Women on Their Own in New Jersey and then added the task of organizing and taking trips to Switzerland for those who were part of the ministry, and she also wanted to travel more abroad.

* * * * *

During this time of trip planning and working with Women on Their Own, Monique's mother died of bone cancer on her birthday, March 3, 1992, at the age of 91. She had been living in Interlaken, Switzerland, and had been extremely frail for some time. It was another loss in Monique's life, but somehow this was easier to handle knowing that her mother had lived a long, productive life. The loss of her mother was also easier to take because Monique was at a healthier place in her own life. She did not feel the devastation she felt when other deaths or losses had taken place earlier in her life. It was right to go to Switzerland and bury her mother. The family buried her in a little cemetery outside Interlaken next to her husband who had passed away 28 years before.

* * * * *

In the early years of Ferne and Monique's friendship, the two women decided it would be an encouragement to connect the widows in the United States with the widows in Uganda. The idea was based on the verses in 2 Corinthians 1:3–5 where it says that God is the God of all comfort. Comfort comes from *com*, which means to go forward, and *fort*, which means strength. Together the word means to go forward in strength. This pen pal idea was hopefully going to allow one widow to comfort another widow through correspondence. Eleanor had helped with this idea and knew how to use the computer. She taught Ferne and Monique how to set the pen pal system up on a computer. Ferne did not have much office experience, but Monique had a background in administration. Working together, the pen pal ministry began.

At that time, Eleanor became ill. Monique traveled to Washington, DC to visit Eleanor and Ferne, who lived six months in the DC area and six months in Uganda. Monique continued pairing up widows through the women of WOTO and the widows in Uganda. She enjoyed the work, and it was fulfilling to be of some assistance to Ferne. Hearing the stories of Uganda from Ferne, Monique realized how encompassing the job was that Ferne was doing there. Monique did not own a computer at the time and had to rent one. She said the computer was as big as a washing machine and didn't even fit on the table.

In August 1992, Eleanor lost her battle with cancer. Monique was familiar enough with what Ferne was doing that she took over the work Eleanor had been doing. In 1993, Ferne was appreciating the work Monique was doing in the United States. She asked Monique if she wanted to come to Africa and help on that side of the world. She could be doing the administrative work in Uganda, and it would help Ferne tremendously. Monique's answer was always the same. "Africa? No! Never!"

After wrestling with Ferne's invitation, Monique began to feel confused. She had no desire to go to Africa. Europe and America were where she was most comfortable, and she felt she was meeting a need and doing what God wanted her to do right where she was. She had no burning need or desire to change things. But God began to work in her. The confusion was getting stronger. She decided to talk to the chairperson at her church who was the head of missions. What should she do? Why should she go? Many questions were swirling around, which seemed to suggest it would be best to stay where she was.

As they sat down to discuss the subject, the advice was simply "you won't know unless you go." She responded, "I guess I'll pack my bags and go for a visit. What could it hurt?" It was now September 1993. In January 1994, Monique headed to Uganda for a three-month visit. In Monique's French-American accent she continued her story.

"I skeptically agreed to go. Ferne talked me into going for three months so I could get a feel for the place. As soon as I stepped off the plane, I wanted to turn around and go home. My sense of smell was assaulted, the poverty was overwhelming, and the heat—this was no place for me. I decided to give it a chance, mostly because I didn't want to look like a weakling."

Ferne was there to pick her up at the airport in Entebbe, Uganda. They loaded up the car and began to drive toward Kampala. As they drove, Monique looked around and saw the poverty, dirt, garbage, filth in the streets, and people selling food right next to the trash. Monique told Ferne, "Put me back on the plane." Ferne just kept driving.

The road from Entebbe to Jinja was filled with a variety of life and nature. The road went through Kampala, the big, busy, bustling capital with many people from all walks of life. It was overcrowded, and many people were very busy and pushy to get where they were going. That did not help Monique's level of comfort in any way.

The next section of the road to Jinja was very beautiful and tranquil. Once the women left Kampala, the journey began to take on a different flavor. "I was sitting in the car and about halfway to Jinja," Monique recalled, "and something came over me." She had a wave of complete peace about being in Africa.

Once they arrived in Jinja and settled in, they began to get to work. Widow's Might assisted the widows who could read and write. These were the women involved in the pen pal ministry with Monique's group in New Jersey. Ferne and Monique went to out-of-the-way villages to bring letters of encouragement to the widows. During these trips, the two women noticed other widows who could not read or write and continued with the life they knew.

Monique and Ferne began to discuss what they could do for widows who were not literate. They decided to help them by giving more farming tools to them so they could increase what they were already doing. The hoes and seeds helped them with what was already growing. Now the widows could sell the excess food to help their families. What seemed to be a slow start for Ferne and Monique turned out to multiply among the widow circles. Ferne and Monique continued doing this for quite a while.

Then, of course, there were the widows' children. These children needed school fees. The ministry would pay for the oldest child to attend school. Things began to multiply as they checked on the orphans and their schooling as well as the farming projects. The Widow's Might office was a support system for these women to group together and support each other. Monique and Ferne visited these groups throughout the area, which included going to some very remote places. These journeys never seemed to bother Ferne as she sat on dirt floors amidst bugs and things, ate the people's food, and encouraged these women. Monique went with Ferne on these visits and discovered that she enjoyed the widows. It did take her a while to get used to some of the situations that Ferne seemed so natural with. In fact, Monique told me she never was as good as Ferne was in some of the authentic African situations.

Monique and Ferne worked side by side with all the aspects of the ministry in Uganda. With Monique's background in accounting, she was able to organize and help in many ways. Of course, during that time, the women became even closer as friends. However, the time for them to go back to the States had come, and Monique was ready to go. The plan for Monique was to work on the US side to match up women in the States with the Ugandan women to be encouragers through writing letters to the African women and raising support.

The two women left Uganda in April 1994. On the way, they stopped in Switzerland to visit the place where Ferne's husband had gone years ago to study French before he went to minister in Africa. Ferne loved visiting Monique's friends and family before they headed back for Ferne's six-month stay in the United States that she took every year.

Once Monique was back in the States, she felt like there was now a place in her heart for the people in Africa. The two women traveled to churches in the States explaining what they were doing, and Ferne introduced Monique to the congregations as her ministry partner. Monique was ready to make the permanent address change. Ferne's ministry was under Global Outreach International, and Monique committed to join Global and be a missionary to widows in Uganda.

It was time to get everything ready for the move. Monique needed to sell things, sort through things she would keep, and decide what to throw away. Moving is never easy, but one thing Monique remembered was how difficult it had been for her mother to let go of the things she had accumulated throughout her life. She had watched her mother agonize over leaving many things she could not take with her to the nursing home in Switzerland. Monique did not want to be like her mother in that way. Things are things, although they still are our connection to our lives.

Monique had two homes she needed to pack up and sell. After going through everything, she narrowed down all her possessions to seven trunks. It was hard to give up some of the treasures she had worked so hard for during her life. She was a cello player and had a beautiful cello. Ever since the accident when she broke her neck, Monique had not been able to play the cello. Her wrists had been damaged, which made it impossible to hold the bow. She knew she could not take her cello to Africa and that she could get a decent amount of money for it. She took it to a shop for an appraisal, and she was right. It was worth a lot of money since it was made in France. The shop bought the cello from her and planned to auction it off. As she began to leave, the shopkeeper asked if she wanted to stay for the auction. Something hit her, and she couldn't stay and watch what she had so treasured be put on an auction block. Selling it was hard enough. Monique declined the offer and walked on.

She began to see a bigger picture, and God was also giving her the peace that passed all her previous understanding about life. God had helped her loosen her grip on the things that had connected her to her life in Europe and the United States. Now it was time to walk on into another chapter. God would be there to hold her hand and walk with her. The might of God working in widows was engaging her in a way that she had not experienced before. Uganda was now beginning to sound like home.

CHAPTER TWENTY-FIVE

Atrocities of Evil

On my first trip to Rwanda with Monique in 2008, I learned more about Rwandan history. I was overwhelmed. I had no words. I felt like I was in some kind of shock, not able to process or make any sense of what was around me. Monique and I were the only ones driving around and seeing sights. It was quiet, haunting, holy.

As we walked around, we saw a little church that was set aside as a memorial to the conflict that took place in 1994. It was set back from the road and music could be heard coming from it. The singing voices were praising God. My heart was trying hard to understand how the past and the present wrestled with each other. I have come to understand that when horrible atrocities happen in life, it's not a matter of God allowing a certain event to take place but Satan who must be much more evil than what I can imagine for him to wreak this kind of havoc on mankind. I was beginning to get a glimpse of how evil Satan can be.

While in Kigali, I went to a genocide museum. It was well put together and did help me understand Rwandan history to a point.

I felt a deep heaviness as I read descriptions of people who had lived through that hell. There were depictions of people crying out for anyone to help, for any kind of rescue, for someone to stop the mayhem. I felt like I was looking at hell.

The human voices who suffered from these crimes against humanity could no longer cry out. I sensed how beautiful God is to give mankind hope amid this kind of evil. As much as Satan wants to keep Rwandans in this horrible past, God put a song of hope in their hearts.

I thought back to that time in history and remembered what I was doing at that time. Although I couldn't help then, I was compelled now to read about it and search out ways to become involved in whatever was stirring in my heart.

As I left the museum, I seemed to feel a personal call to action. If others in our world would only find and help ministries and nonprofits that are honest and truly do good around the world or in our backyards. If many could just get involved financially or physically, or both. There is always a crisis going on somewhere. We are blessed people; we can bless others. We can help lift the load or burden from the helpless. That's what these Rwandan people were hoping for—someone to hear them. Sadly, all they felt and heard was rejection. *It's your own battle. It's your own country's deep-rooted problems.* The rest of the world continued on their paths while the Rwandans suffered through this conflict that left a broken, destroyed country. I'm reminded of a verse in Genesis 50:20 where Joseph had his set of troubles, but he saw that God intended it for good. Satan's goal is for evil, but God's is for good. What a beautiful contrast!

When I saw the horrible state Rwanda was left in after those 100 days in 1994, God touched my heart and encouraged me to do even the smallest act and be used by God to touch these people who had been in the midst of evil itself.

We drove back to our hotel in Kigali with heavy hearts. Monique explained a little more about how difficult it had been for the people of Rwanda. The strength of the human spirit was being revealed to me every day. And I was about to see this strength lived out in the people I came to know and love in Rwanda.

CHAPTER TWENTY-SIX

Monique Finds a New Address

F erne and Monique were excited to be working together in Africa. They began right away with the work that faced them in Jinja. Monique was experienced with administrative work and had a heart for widows. She and Ferne were working well together, and the ministry grew. It was late 1994, and things were going well amidst the hard work that all ministries encounter. Just to the southwest of Uganda was Rwanda, a little French-speaking country.

Ferne and Monique were living very near the Kenyan border of Uganda, and they were not aware of the conflict that had taken place in Rwanda just months before from April 7 through July 7, 1994. They continued to work among the widows and their children in the Jinja area. Their work was divided between working in Uganda and traveling to the United States to inform others of the ministry and how they could become involved. There was also the fundraising part that all ministries need to be constantly attending to. So needless to say, there were trips back and forth between the States and Uganda so the work could continue.

These women were not ignorant of the troubles going on so close to their African homes. In 1994, major crises had begun to play out around the world. There would be conflicts in Sudan, Afghanistan, Myanmar, Burma, Cambodia, Somalia, Croatia, Bosnia, and Rwanda, to name just a few. The world seemed to be having issues on many continents. The crisis in Rwanda, the tiny country to the southwest of Uganda, was just that—another crisis.

No one seemed to understand or know what was happening in Rwanda or to what extent. Monique began to have a sense that God was putting Rwanda on her heart. She knew the country's business language was French, and French was Monique's first language. She began to pray about what, if anything, she could do. Surely there would be widows there, and maybe she could help. She chose not to say anything to anyone, including Ferne, but continued to pray over the matter.

It wasn't until January 1997 when Monique and Ferne were walking along a beach in Florida that Monique shared with Ferne what she had been thinking regarding Rwanda. A thought kept coming to her, but she kept shooing it away. Once she told Ferne, they prayed about it. Ferne thought that it was at least worth investigating to see what might come of it. Monique had been praying about this for more than two years, since the horrible conflict in 1994, and now she would continue to pray, but now with Ferne. Since Monique was from France and Switzerland, she decided to make a stop in Europe before returning to Uganda. She could contact friends and family there, tell them about the situation in Rwanda, and see if anyone was interested in supporting a new ministry under Widow's Might. Monique also wanted to find some French-speaking partners who would be willing to write to Rwandan widows.

Various friends and family in France and Switzerland became interested in this new idea. Monique asked Ferne to come to Nancy, France, so she could introduce her to friends and family. Now the people in France and Switzerland could hear about the ministry of Widow's Might directly from Ferne.

After their trip to Europe, the two women had not yet decided to open up a ministry in Rwanda. They continued their ministry with the widows in Uganda. For two full months in early 1997, Monique prayed about Rwanda. She felt her insides churn with conflict. *Do I concentrate on the ministry that I felt called to do here in Uganda? Do I step out and help the people in Rwanda? Do I abandon Ferne here in Uganda? Do I have any support to start a ministry? Do I know anything about Rwanda? Do I know how to start a ministry?*

The questions that nagged at her soul continued throughout the month of March. Then, on April 9, 1997, Monique was reading her Bible. "Lead me, Lord, in your righteousness because of my enemies—make your way straight before me" (Ps. 5:8). She shut her Bible and felt peace. She wanted the straightway. "So God, you need to make the straightway very clear."

With this deep sense of being compelled to follow the straight path God had in mind, she left her room and headed to the kitchen. A minute later, Ferne came into the kitchen and started talking. She suggested that she and Monique go to the Rwandan Embassy in Kampala to inquire about getting visas to visit the country. The car was damaged, but friends were going into Kampala that day, and they could get a ride with them. Monique, of course, agreed. This was very clear now, and she had no doubt what the straightway was. It seemed to Monique about as clear as it could get. They headed to the Embassy and were able to get the required visas. They both were on a plane two days later.

Monique felt that God was leading them, but from the outside, it wouldn't have made sense to go into a country so ravaged by conflict and begin setting things up. They didn't have any direct contacts there and no real deep understanding of what was going on, what needs the country had, how to start, where to go, or what to do. Monique remembered the many times God had not exposed everything that needed to be figured out before He asked her to act. So here she was, going with her instinct and a sense of peace that God was doing the leading.

Once they arrived in Kigali, Rwanda's capital, they knew of one person to contact. They set up meetings with this person who helped them arrange several meetings with others in Kigali. The country was trying to put everything back together before they could even look past themselves and allow others to come in and help. During Ferne and Monique's two days in Kigali, they met a widow, and she would be the one who would help get things started.

As Ferne and Monique headed back to Uganda, they realized how huge this work was going to be. They had seen firsthand the devastation and insurmountable needs of the people of Rwanda. They continued meeting the needs of the widows in Uganda while putting together plans for the Widow's Might branch in Rwanda.

Monique traveled to Quebec, Canada, to see if she could get sponsors to start the ministry. She wanted to start with 18 sponsors. Each one would write to one widow and encourage her as a sister in Christ. At the first church she visited, she received 11 sponsors. She was excited! At the next church, she received exactly seven! She now had her 18 sponsors.

Monique moved to Kigali with a permanent new address, and the Rwandan branch of Widow's Might officially opened in January 1998.

CHAPTER TWENTY-SEVEN

Jean de la Paix
(John of the Peace)

When Monique moved to Kigali, she met a boy there who worked at the pastor's home as a gatekeeper. He was in charge of opening and closing the gate whenever someone came to the home. When Monique visited the pastor's home, she always noticed the boy's servant's heart. He had a great attitude and loved to help others. Monique decided to have him do some small jobs for her. He enjoyed working for Monique no matter how small the job was and did his work with an infectious smile.

Monique noticed the potential in Jean de la Paix and wanted to know more about him. She asked the pastor about his background and his education. The boy had little education and no family. He used to walk three to four hours to school each day but had no time to study. He was always extremely tired. Jean de la Paix was also not a boy but a young man in his late teens. Monique wanted to help him get his education, so she set it up so he could go to school. Jean de la Paix was eager to learn from anyone.

Once he was back in school, Monique checked to see how he was doing. She found out he wasn't doing very well; in fact, he wasn't doing well at all. He had received only a 42 percent score on his exam. When the ministry helped students, they had to maintain decent grades, and 42 percent was not considered decent. Jean de la Paix begged for one more chance to go to school. Monique looked into putting him in a boarding school. He received his chance and brought his grades up to 87 percent. He stayed in school to finish secondary school. By the time he finished, he was in his late 20s.

Jean de la Paix stayed in contact with Monique even after the ministry moved to Butare, a town in the southern part of Rwanda. He finished school in 2011 but did not get a job. He did odd jobs around Kigali and then in 2013 moved to Butare to help with the ministry. The ministry was making sunflower oil, and Monique put Jean de la Paix in charge of the process. He had also learned English and helped whenever anyone came to teach English in the workshops.

I met Jean de la Paix in the summer of 2013. He wanted to be baptized and had invited Monique and me to the baptism. We walked down to the river where many people had gathered for the event. The first person into the water was an older gentleman who walked around in the river to make sure it was safe. Then the pastor entered the water wearing a white robe. When it was Jean de la Paix's turn, he waded into the river, was baptized, and emerged out of the water with a shining smile.

We walked back to the area where he lived and had arranged to have food for his guests. He was excited to have us visit his home. We ate some food and took many pictures. It had been 16 years since Monique had first met him in Kigali. His spirit was still filled with gratitude, and it was very contagious. Caring for others can turn a person's life around, and that's what it did for Jean de la Paix.

CHAPTER TWENTY-EIGHT

Ministering in Rwanda

When Monique went to Rwanda, the plan was to do the same type of ministry that was going on in Uganda. She first began ministering to the widows she was getting to know. Some of them had gone through an incredible amount of trauma and unbelievable pain and suffering. They were in dire need of support to get back on their feet.

Monique started meetings with the widows for support and encouragement. She started by telling them about the Word of God. The ministry also held seminars where widows could come from all over Rwanda and stay from Monday through Friday. The place Monique rented had rooms with 12 bunk beds. The first seminars had 24 to 30 in attendance. The women ate well and went to workshops to learn about their motivational gifts. The workshops were very successful, and soon Monique was holding seminars all over Rwanda.

James 1:27 states that pure religion is to help the widows and the orphans. While ministering to widows, Monique became aware of the overwhelming problem of the orphans in the country—the street kids. She had met some of them in Kigali. These kids had lost everyone and everything. They had little to no education, no families, and no skills. Some of them were even living in the local dumps. They were on drugs and alcohol just to survive. These damaging, coping practices helped them forget their pain and their hunger.

After praying and trying to think of something that would help with their plight, Monique decided these young people needed something to do. She thought about starting workshops for them to teach them how to sew, carve wood, make greeting cards designed with banana bark, do carpentry, weave baskets, and more. The Rwandan people are very artistic by nature, and these youth were able to learn a skill and turn it into a job. Many of the street kids came, mastered a skill, and learned about Christ. They began to have some of their lives restored to them.

The ministry rented homes that housed four kids per house. There were mattresses and dishes in the homes, and once the kids made some money, they paid the ministry back little by little for the mattresses. That helped the kids learn to be responsible. Monique followed the Salvation Army's slogan: Soup, Soap, Salvation. You first need to feed them, and then clean them to give them dignity and worth. Finally, you present the gospel. How can dejected, hungry youth hear that God loves them when they are in such dire conditions? When the youth came to the workshops, the ministry provided food for them, followed by work and the gospel—the soup, the soap, and the salvation.

The widows throughout all the regions of Rwanda had many children, and Monique thought it would be good to get them together. She had meetings three times a year so the children of widows could come together and support each other. They came from every area of Rwanda, and at least one in every region would become a leader of their area. They would ask other youth to go to a meeting in Kigali. The ministry gave the leaders bus fare for these orphans so they could come to Kigali and attend the meeting. Sometimes the ministry rented a bus to bring the groups to the meeting.

The meeting was an all-day affair. It started at 10:00 in the morning. The youth sat in areas designated for the region where they lived. There were singing, choirs, traditional Rwandan dances, and food. The young leaders were responsible to organize their group to sing, dance, or perform a skit. After the group sang and prayed, Monique brought them a message about God's love. Many of these youth came to know God at those meetings. At about 2:00 p.m., it was time for lunch, and the ministry provided food for all the kids.

In the same compound where Monique lived in Kigali was a lady from Switzerland who had a shelter where these street kids could go to stay off the streets. The two women began to get to know each other. The Swiss woman thought it would be great for some of the street kids in her area to come to the youth meetings so they could hear about God. The Swiss woman was under a limited contract with a church that followed the government rule that no child can be sheltered in an orphanage once they reach the age of 18. Monique had gotten to know and care about these orphans and was concerned about where they would go after they turned 18.

Monique purchased a guesthouse with the idea that these 18-year-old orphans would have a place to go instead of going back to the streets. Without the guesthouse, the youth would have to find a place to live, sometimes with a distant relative or friend, and then come to work to learn a particular skill. Sadly, the guesthouse never opened since Monique had to go back to the States.

On the day of the workshops, the youth woke up early and then walked for half an hour to four hours just to get to the workshops. A typical day at the workshops started with a breakfast of sorghum, an oatmeal type of grain provided by the ministry, a Bible verse and teaching, and a time of prayer. Then they began working in their particular area. At noon, they stopped for lunch, which was also provided by the ministry. Then they were back to work for the afternoon. The workshop ended around 4:30 p.m. so the youth had time to walk back to the places they lived.

The workshops provided the dignity these former street kids needed by teaching them a skill they could use to provide for themselves. They were paid for each item they made. This was not a place to show up and not work. Monique told the youth that if they didn't work, they didn't eat or get paid. The workshops provided a safe place for them, and they also heard about a God who loves them. Many of them turned to God for their salvation, healing, and worth.

The need for a new name for the ministry was now quite evident. Widow's Might was not just dealing with widows, so the name Youth Might came into existence. Youth Might would end up ministering to more than 150 young Rwandans who were former street kids.

Monique had developed programs to help widows sustain themselves, and now she was helping these precious youth who had lived through such atrocities know their value through Christ. Lives were changed—lives of marginalized people who would typically end up in human trafficking or drug trade just to survive. Monique was simply a saint to both the widows and the youth she worked so hard to help.

CHAPTER TWENTY-NINE

A Boy Named Miracle

Ayouth who was about 13 years old heard about the Youth Might workshops and came to check them out. He was usually high on drugs and would come for a day and then be missing for a few days. Monique asked some of the others to find him. Many times, they found him in the dumps both drunk and high and would bring him back where he was given food and could work a bit. He seemed like he wanted to work, but he was trapped by the drugs and alcohol he used to numb the trauma and pain he had endured when he was just a child. He also could not read or write because he had never gone to school.

He began to come more regularly, and Monique found out that his name was Immanuel. He became a consistent part of the workshops making greeting cards. He was showing promise with his artistic skills. He later changed his name to Matthew.

While working at the workshops, Matthew received the most consistent care he had ever received. He was given two meals a day and was learning a skill. And then there were the times of Bible reading and prayer before work began. He was hearing God's Word, and the people at the workshops were becoming like family.

Once the young adults involved with the workshops gained enough skills to find jobs elsewhere, they branched out on their own or with a couple of friends to find work in bigger cities. Matthew was able to leave the workshops and find work elsewhere. He was stable and wanted to live out his life well.

A few years later, Monique ran into him and asked how he was doing. When she referred to him as Matthew, he smiled a big, infectious smile and said that wasn't his name. His name now was Miracle. This miracle all started when Monique reached out to him, a kid who had nothing going for him. Now he goes by Miracle.

CHAPTER THIRTY

Life Changes

Monique worked in Rwanda and Ferne in Uganda, but they also traveled back and forth to help each other out. Both ministries were making progress and changing lives for the better. In 2000 during a time when the ladies were together, Ferne was treating a sore on her heel. She later left to go to the States to attend a wedding, and a couple of months later, Monique picked her up at the airport. She noticed that the sore still had not healed and wondered why Ferne did not have it looked at in the States while she was there. Another friend told Ferne to go to the clinic in Kampala. It was now early August. The medical staff couldn't find anything that seemed alarming, so they sent her home. Along with the problem with her heel, she was experiencing a lot of pain throughout her body.

Ferne was growing more and more concerned with her health, and she was not feeling well. Those around her could tell that she was quite ill. She left for the States around the middle of September so she could have a thorough exam. After the exam and tests, it was confirmed that Ferne had melanoma. The cancer had spread to the rest of her body. She didn't have long to live. Ferne passed away in December 2000.

Of course, this was devastating to Monique. She wasn't a stranger to death, but it was still something she never got used to. Monique returned to Africa to direct both ministries in Uganda and Rwanda. The ministry workers in both countries rallied around her and did what was necessary to continue the ministry. They had learned to rely on God, but now it was paramount for their faith and reliance on God to carry on the ministries. Monique did the same. As she had done many times before when disaster struck her life, she pushed on, looked straight ahead, and took the next step required of her.

Going back and forth between countries became a norm for Monique. "You do what you need to do," Monique explained. "There's no one else to rely on. God will equip you with what you need at the time." She had shared with me the idea that life is like a suitcase.

"When you pack for a trip, you plan and pack the items you think you will need for your destination. Life is like that. However, God packs your suitcase. All of the things that happen in your life will be useful once you get to that specific destination. For instance, when I was taken from my parents when I was eight years old, I had that sense of what it's like to be an orphan. During that time, I didn't understand it. Even later in my life, I couldn't understand why I went through such a time of anguish and being alone and scared. Now when I work with orphans, I can somewhat relate to their pain. God knew what was in the future and had packed my suitcase accordingly so I would be prepared for what I am doing now."

Monique went on to say that she didn't believe God plans these difficulties in life but does use them for His glory when a believer allows God to use them. Once again, Monique had to walk on, even when it did not seem possible and wasn't how she would have planned things. It was time to get dressed and take the next steps.

CHAPTER THIRTY-ONE

The Son of a Widow Becomes a Child of God

Janvier was fatherless, and he was living on the streets. His mother was part of the Widow's Might group, and it was through that contact that Monique got to know Janvier. She invited him to one of the meetings, and he felt great peace being there. When Monique invited him to another gathering, he decided to go. During one of the gatherings, Janvier signed up for a seminar called "Discover Your God-Given Gift." Not knowing what would take place, he learned about who God is and gave his life to Christ.

Monique had given him a Bible with instructions to read at least one word a day. Janvier did more than that. He read a lot of words every day and began to understand more about Christ, which gave him much-needed direction. His faith grew, and Monique knew he needed a skill so he could work. She sent him to a trade school where he learned to be an electrician. He was a good student, but he felt God had something more for him.

Janvier loved to share Christ with others. He started prayer groups in high schools and became known as a preacher. He worked as an electrician but was always asking God what he wanted him to do. In 2012, Janvier felt God calling him to mission work. He applied and was accepted to a six-month program, and he would be going to Asia. Janvier felt God had made a way for him to go.

In Asia, he worked to develop his talent in film. He enjoyed telling stories of God's redemption, so films were a great avenue to do just that. As he trained and shared Christ with others, he showed great compassion for others who did not know Christ. Janvier's heart burned to share Christ with as many people as possible. God had rescued him, and he wanted others to know this redemption too.

Janvier was quick to give God all the praise for what he did in his life, but he also realized that Monique was the one God had used to help him start his journey with Christ. He shared how thankful he was that Monique heeded God's voice and became obedient to come and serve him in Africa. Janvier became a missionary who would serve God wherever he was called. The ripple effect that started with Monique saying yes to God had transformed Janvier from an orphan to a child of God.

CHAPTER THIRTY-TWO

More Life Changes

Now that Monique was running two ministries in two countries, help from the States sounded like a welcome idea. Monique's oldest granddaughter decided to come over to help. Of course, that thrilled Monique. The two of them worked together, traveled back and forth between Uganda and Rwanda, and enjoyed their familial relationship. While her granddaughter was there, she fell in love with a young man from Rwanda. Wedding plans began.

In May 2002, Monique and her granddaughter went to Europe to visit some supporters of the ministry. Monique thought it would be a good opportunity to line up some doctors' visits while they were in France. Monique's granddaughter was able to get an appointment, which was usually difficult since most appointments had to be scheduled months in advance. The evening before the appointment, Monique thought she found a lump on herself. The thought came to her that she needed to have it looked at before returning to Rwanda. She knew how difficult it was to get appointments in these French clinics, but she decided to call anyway. To Monique's surprise, there was one appointment available. She knew God had made a way for her.

The doctor examined Monique and concluded that she had cancer. The medical staff told her that if she wanted to beat it, she *must* go to the United States. It appeared that the cancer was highly invasive. It would take too long for Monique to receive the necessary treatments and care in France.

Unbelievably, Monique didn't fall apart even though she was very familiar with cancer and what it does. She made an appointment in the States with her doctor. Then she flew back to Rwanda with her granddaughter and got things settled there before she would leave for the States.

Her doctor's appointment was in June 2002, and the doctors wanted to do a biopsy. After the biopsy, they confirmed that Monique had breast cancer. She would need a full mastectomy and chemotherapy to defeat cancer. On July 22, 2002, Monique had the surgery. The surgeons found that one breast was filled with cancer. When she came out of surgery, she found out that her only sister, Anne Marie, who lived in Maine, had died that day of a blood clot.

The news was devastating to Monique. It had not even been two years since Ferne had died, and now her little sister had finished her walk on this earth. It was Monique's ability to walk forward with a strength that allowed her not to give up. The Bible tells us that the God of all comfort comforts us in our troubles (2 Cor. 1:3–4). It was evident that this was where Monique was getting her strength.

Once she gained back her physical strength after surgery, Monique flew back to Rwanda and stayed one month to put everything in order for the time she would be in the States to complete her chemotherapy. She worked hard to make sure those involved with the ministry would be taken care of and that ministering to the people would continue even though she was not there. That was the type of person she was, someone who took care of others before she took care of herself.

* * * * *

The year before, in October 2001, a church in Canada that supported the ministries of Youth Might and Widow's Might asked Monique to be the keynote speaker at a retreat they were planning for October 2002. Monique was very familiar with this church since she had been there several times to visit, and she had been giving them regular updates about the ministry. In March 2002, they had given her the title of the retreat—Life Is Beautiful. Monique accepted the invitation and planned to be there for the retreat later that year. This was all before she was diagnosed with cancer. Was this a coincidence?

Now it was September 2002, and the chemotherapy treatments were set to take place. There is a lot of information about cancer treatments and what patients go through. It's a dark and difficult journey. It was no different for Monique. She would have the first of many treatments 13 days before she was scheduled to speak at the conference in Canada.

The treatment left her feeling extremely tired and terribly sick. The medical staff that prepped her for the surgery and the cancer treatment plan told her that this was to be expected. They also told her that about the 13th day after the first treatment, her hair would begin to fall out. A friend had told Monique she should get a wig for when her hair fell out. So they went together and picked out a wig.

The retreat was scheduled to start on October 4. By September 30, Monique was feeling strong enough to go and felt she could do this. Her strength had returned, she wasn't feeling really sick, and she still had her hair.

Driving the 13 hours to Canada gave her time to reflect on the topic of her presentation and go over the notes she had prepared. She had these three main points for the weekend: Are you surprised when you suffer? Suffering is only for a while. All things work together for good to those who love God. She definitely could speak from experience.

The retreat started on Friday evening, and everything was going according to schedule. Saturday morning came, and as she was showering, her hair came out in handfuls. Monique seemed so strong, but losing her hair was just too much. She broke down and cried.

"I never thought of myself as a vain person, but when you lose your hair, especially for a woman, I couldn't hold it back. It seemed that all my physical dignity was gone. I had to rely on who I was in Christ. I knew all the Bible verses and talks that go with that idea, but I just fell apart."

It was time to use the wig. She was so appreciative of her friend who insisted that she take a wig just in case the inevitable happened. And it had happened.

The retreat continued, and Monique shared from the depths of her heart. Here she was in the midst of some of her deepest pain, literally and emotionally. It was hard for her to handle being the keynote speaker as she was walking through her own suffering. Relying on her notes, she continued to speak, knowing that even this suffering was only for a while. She knew God was with her. She shared in those moments how very real God is. She finished the retreat and headed back to the States for more treatment.

* * * * *

Going back to face more chemotherapy was not something she looked forward to. What she did know was that it wouldn't do any good to worry or fret about it. What was facing her in the future was scary, real, and painful, but she knew she needed to always move in a forward motion. She chose to engage in the life she had rather than run from it and all its pain.

When she returned for treatment, the doctors found that her blood count wasn't high enough for the next chemotherapy treatment. She needed to wait a week. When the time came for her treatment, they planned to give her two types of chemo. Chemotherapy, as we know, is designed to kill cancer cells. To Monique, it felt like it would kill her. After the treatment, she couldn't eat because she was so sick. All she could do was sleep. This went on for 10 days. She lost weight and any kind of meaningful life. Her daughter told her later that she looked like death. Once she recovered enough, it was time to repeat the process. Monique had to keep her eyes on God. There was nothing else she could do.

The treatments continued for about seven months until April 2003. They were finally over, and hopefully, so was the cancer. Monique was still weak, but the doctors told her that they were sure they had gotten all the cancer cells and that she was cancer-free.

Weak and fatigued, Monique could now only rest. She was cleared to resume her life, so she decided to return to Uganda and Rwanda and get back to work. "I knew I needed to get back to work, and I was tired," she shared. "But I decided that you can rest on any of God's continents!" As she reflected on her battle with cancer, she shared what Billy Graham once said, "The will of God will not take us where the grace of God cannot sustain us."[1] So she packed her things, donned her wig, and off she went.

---

1. "Billy Graham Quotes," Goodreads, accessed April 26, 2022, https://www.goodreads.com/quotes/199683-the-will-of-god-will-not-take-us-where-the.

CHAPTER THIRTY-THREE

Rwandan Lives

When I visited Monique for the first time in 2008, we had driven to Kigali and were getting our things put away when Monique received a call from a young man who wanted to come and speak to her about an important issue. In a mere 10 minutes, he showed up at the office.

In walked a tall, handsome young man about 24 or 25 years old. Emmanuel sat down with us and began to speak in his broken English of a desire he had. He said it was time for him to be baptized. In Rwanda, when a person is baptized, people have a party for that person and those closest to them. He wanted to know if he could have his baptism party at the office and if Monique could be there as his family. I could tell that this meant a lot to him. He seemed like a 10-year-old boy looking for affirmation that only a parent can give. To see the twinkle in his eyes spoke volumes.

Emmanuel had only a sister, and they helped each other out as much as they could. He had previously come in contact with Monique, that "white lady who might be able to help him," and his life had begun to change. Monique had become his world. She had taken him in and given him a place to live in one of the rented houses. As Monique got to know Emanuel, she recognized that he had a gift. He was an amazing woodcarver and made beautiful wood sculptures. She hired him to make carvings and teach other young men to do the same. Monique also sent him to school for English. Being a quick learner and a hard worker, Emanuel excelled in his classes. Monique began to see leadership qualities in this young man.

During his time in the ministry, he had come to know Christ as his Savior. As time went on, he and the other young people began to trust Monique and realized she was not there to take advantage of them as other people had done in the past.

God does take the brokenhearted and restore them by giving them hope and a future. Here is a young man who had gone through horrific things that no child or adult should go through and yet accepted the God of life when he was introduced to him. Monique was used to bringing the good news to many of these people. They highly respected and honored her. These young people of Youth Might saw her as a parent and, in some cases, the only earthly parent they had.

Later, I was talking to Emmanuel about how well he teaches. I was complimenting him on the way he instructs others and the beautiful products he produces. As I was speaking, he pointed up and said, "It's all God." I wish I had a picture of his face as he said those words.

CHAPTER THIRTY-FOUR

Can Life Get Any More Difficult?

Monique arrived in Rwanda in a wheelchair. Life was resuming for her as much as possible after her battle with cancer. Her granddaughter was getting married, so along with running the ministries in Uganda and Rwanda, Monique had a wedding to plan. The wedding took place, and a year later, they had a sweet baby. Now Monique was a great-grandmother. The couple soon moved to the States to work on their education.

Monique was getting used to traveling back and forth between the two African countries. She also had reliable help with drivers and staff from both Uganda and Rwanda. Many times, Monique needed to go by car on the African roads between the two countries. The trip could take 12 to 15 hours, and Monique didn't have anyone to travel with her. Driving that long on those roads was not always safe. Monique asked around to see if anyone would be able to go with her, and as always, God sent someone right at the moment she needed them.

In August 2004, Monique needed to go to the States. She typically made one trip per year for fundraising and speaking engagements. Flights to the States consisted of an eight-hour flight to Europe and then a transatlantic flight of about seven hours. When Monique was a child, she always struggled with restless legs. As she aged, this restlessness became known as restless leg syndrome. Sitting for more than 15 hours in a plane would drive her crazy, so she walked around a great deal on the flight. As she was sharing this story with me, she jokingly said, "I don't know why I have to pay to fly since I walk the entire way to Europe and America!" Even with her restless leg syndrome, she took things in stride and was able to laugh about her ailments. It was now time to board a plane and head to the States for fundraising, commitments, and a variety of appointments she had lined up.

While she was in the States, her granddaughter and grandson-in-law were in the middle of a move. They were moving to Florida, and they asked Monique if she could help them. Moving day was August 21, 2004. Since her granddaughter and her baby had already left in another vehicle, the grandson-in-law and Monique drove down the coast together. In North Carolina, Monique was driving with the cruise control on, going around 70 miles per hour when a pickup suddenly whipped in front of her and cut her off. The driver of the truck kept tapping his brakes and then suddenly stopped right in front of Monique. She saw that the right lane was empty and veered over and began to fishtail. As she tried to brake, she noticed that the brakes didn't work. The car plowed into three trees on the side of the road and stopped.

Her grandson-in-law called the police who eventually came. As they sat there waiting for help, they didn't think there was much damage. Monique was trapped in the car since her car door was right up against a tree. The airbag had engaged and was holding her in one place. She felt fine. Her grandson-in-law had a broken bone and a burned eye due to the airbag but didn't feel any life-threatening injuries.

Once the emergency response teams got there, they realized they needed to cut the car to get Monique out. As soon as they got her out, she passed out. What she didn't know was that the airbag was holding her together. She had massive internal injuries. She ended up in a coma with life support for six days. While she was in the coma, they realized she needed surgery on her colon and her trachea. Before they were able to do the surgeries, the hospital had some other emergency surgeries that had come up. When they finally operated on her colon, they didn't have to remove all of it. It had healed enough on its own, and Monique wouldn't have to live without her colon. Her trachea had also healed enough so they didn't need to do the surgery they originally thought they would have to do. However, there were other issues, and she ended up having three surgeries followed by six days in intensive care where she had to rely on a breathing machine. Once released from ICU, she remained in North Carolina for a month. Later, she was airlifted to New Jersey where she was admitted to a rehabilitation center. Monique also had a terrible burn on her arm, but it had healed on its own. The burn was bad enough that the medical staff thought she would require skin grafting. By now it was near the end of September, and she wouldn't come out of rehab until it was nearly Christmas.

Her grandson-in-law had to have three surgeries and treatment for the burn to his eye. Both Monique and her grandson-in-law felt extremely grateful to be alive after what they had gone through. When Monique was released from the hospital and rehab, the doctors told her they had given her a 50 percent chance to live. She explained that she hadn't felt much pain after the accident. Maybe it was because she had lived through so many other painful events. She does, however, remember that the doctors counted 159 staples they had used to hold her together during her recovery.

Monique told me that after all her illnesses, surgeries, and accidents, her body looked like a road map of a busy city due to all the scars. Her attitude always amazed me as she pushed on and didn't complain. She believed it was her duty to continue to help others as long as she could and with whatever energy she had. She took each day as a gift even though there were times when her body did not work as well as it once had. The accidents and illnesses had left many scars and physical challenges, but she pressed on and always said, "It's time to get dressed!" She meant it was time to put on the armor of God and do what she could to help others.

After she healed from the accident, Monique "got dressed" and set out to complete the work God had set before her. She packed her bags and headed back to Africa.

CHAPTER THIRTY-FIVE

Jean Pierre and Patrick

We had been in Rwanda, and it was now time to head back to Uganda after being in Kigali for about a week. Monique informed me that we would be taking back two young men. One was Patrick, a 22-year-old former street kid who worked in the workshops. He was an artist and was going to Uganda to hopefully see his brother whom he had not seen for more than a year.

Patrick was extremely shy and didn't know any English or French. On our way, we needed to stop and stay at a hotel in Musaka, Uganda. Through the other young man who interpreted for Patrick, we found out that Patrick was amazed at the softness of the mattress and how good the food was. It was Patrick's first time sleeping on a mattress. He had always slept on a mat on the floor.

Monique had made arrangements for Patrick to meet up with his brother, Jean Pierre, once we arrived in Jinja. They were the only family they had, and both of them had sought out a life and whatever jobs they could find, which had separated them from each other.

The day came for the two of them to meet. Patrick was nervous and decided to go for a run, unbeknownst to us. The time was getting closer when Jean Pierre would arrive. We called for Patrick and looked around the compound to no avail. Where could Patrick be? About five minutes before the two were to meet, Patrick came back into the yard. Monique quickly asked him where he had been. He told us through an interpreter that he had to do some sport, or running, to burn off his nervousness.

The time came for Jean Pierre to come. He walked into the office, and the two brothers instantly hugged and laughed. There was much joy in their reunion. Everyone was excited to see the two reunite. I had my camera ready, and as I took pictures of their reunion; the camera caught a light or twinkle in both of their eyes. It was beautiful.

Patrick first met Monique when he came to the workshop to do artwork in Rwanda. She noticed that he was a talented artist. She sent him to art classes where he would learn a certain artistic skill. Because he was so naturally artistic, he became a workshop teacher. He was known for making imigongo art which is made from a clay-like substance that is put on flat wood and shaped into geometric designs and then painted. Rwanda is known for this art that can be found in most restaurants and hotels as part of its décor.

Through an interpreter, I listened to Patrick share how God had changed his life. He talked only about when he had met Monique. As he shared, he explained that he now had a father, and he pointed upward, and he now had a mother, and he pointed to Monique. He went on to explain that now he can rent a place to live and he can buy food. With a big smile on his face, he explained that he could buy clothes and had achieved dignity, a family, and a relationship with God.

His brother, Jean Pierre, was just as beautiful as his younger brother. After the brothers met, Monique had Jean Pierre come back to Rwanda and help in the office. This smart and very conscientious young man had come to know Christ through Monique, and his life had changed.

There was never a dull moment when Monique was working to give these former street kids hope and a future. Even with her own difficulties, she was a champion for these young adults who had lost so much. Now they were being given a chance at a better life, one of dignity and worth.

CHAPTER THIRTY-SIX

On the Move

In 2005, Monique needed a new place to rent for her office and workshops. As she was driving around Kigali, she happened to notice a for rent sign in a neighborhood. It was Friday, and she asked one of the young men to check into it for her. Sure enough, it was available and at a good price. The home belonged to the ambassador to Canada, and he was thrilled to have someone rent the home that would help his people in Rwanda. It all seemed to be directed by God.

The ministry operated out of the house for three years. During that time, Kigali was making many improvements, which included upgrading all the buildings. The new upgrade requirements were making it difficult financially for the ministry. Since there were many non-governmental organizations in Kigali to help the people, Monique thought it might be better if she helped in other areas in Rwanda that were receiving little to no help. Some of these districts were severely impoverished. Maybe the difficulties imposed on buildings in Kigali were a blessing in disguise. Maybe it was time to help in areas that had so little.

Monique began traveling around Rwanda looking for places that could work for the ministry. In 2008, one of the workshop workers came to Monique and informed her of a school that was closed in the Butare district where he had lived. Monique drove to that area and met with the executive secretary of the sector. He listened to her plan to use the school for workshops and agreed to let her use the school for her ministry. The area where the school was located was in a very impoverished area of Rwanda. How could it be any more fitting for the ministry? It was a building that could now be used for workshops. Again, this seemed to be directed by God.

Now to deal with moving the youth of Youth Might to Butare. Would they be willing to move from Kigali to another area? Before they came, Monique would need to arrange housing for them. The same young man who told Monique about the school contacted a man who owned some buildings across the street from the school. The man was willing to rent the buildings to Monique for a fair price. One building would be for the girls, and one would be for the boys. Now it was time to ask the youth if they wanted to move.

Now that the housing and workshops were arranged for the youth, Monique would also need a place to live and operate the office for Widow's Might and Youth Might. Another contact knew of a house for rent in Butare right outside the village where the workshops were located. The house was perfect. There were rooms for office space, her personal space, and a couple of rooms that could be used for guests when they came to visit. This was another answer to prayer.

Once back in Kigali, Monique needed to explain the move and make all the necessary arrangements to transport the youth to Butare. She told the youth the ministry was moving to the Butare area and they were all invited to come. She understood that some might not want to go since they had established their lives in Kigali. Would any of the youth want to come? Monique wasn't sure what was going to happen, but she trusted God to bring the right ones to Butare. She arranged for a bus and told the youth that if they wanted to move, a bus would be at the office on moving day and that they were free to board the bus to go to their new location.

The day came when the bus was parked outside the office. Would anyone be there to take the bus? Monique had already gone to Butare and wondered how many, if any, would be on the bus. She waited at the workshop to welcome the youth as they got off the bus. Still unsure how many would come; she would rejoice in however many youths came. The bus finally arrived and pulled up to the workshop buildings. The door of the bus opened. The youth stepped off to their new life—70 of them.

CHAPTER THIRTY-SEVEN

The Ministry Is Ministering

onique had been working in Rwanda for more than 25 years. She was well-known and respected throughout the country. Every once in a while, she held youth meetings where young people could come and hear the Word of God. Someone told a young man who was not involved with the ministry that he should go and hear this woman. André was not in a good place in his life. He was a university student who had his own sorrows. To help himself make it through life, he had become an alcoholic and was abusing drugs. Begrudgingly, he went that day to hear Monique. He listened. He left. Later, André could not stop thinking of some of the things Monique had said. He decided to email her and talk to her some more about this God she spoke about. He asked if she would meet with him. Monique agreed. When they met, he shared how he had put his hope and trust in Christ based on what she had shared that evening several weeks before. Monique was encouraged to see this young man turn his life around.

One month later, Monique received an email from André asking if Monique could meet with him and some friends to discuss a ministry. Her first response was this— "that's great, but I have *no* money!"

They met on the appointed day in a bar, much to Monique's apprehension. She was expecting to see André and a few others. When she walked in, there were 33 university students there who were excited to start a ministry. The government had cracked down on new ministries starting up in Rwanda, so André needed an existing ministry to partner with. When he became a believer, he had become convicted about doing something for the street kids in his university town. His excitement was contagious, and now his friends at the university all wanted to help out in some way. André looked to Monique for ideas, structure, and ways to go about reaching out to these street kids. They ended up working together under Youth Might to help street kids who were anywhere from eight to 28 years old.

André was a quiet young man with a tender, compassionate heart for those less fortunate than him. He became drug-free and alcohol-free and graduated from the university in May 2012.

In the summer of 2011, I was asked to take some pictures of an event called the Day of the Child that honored children. André wanted his group of street kids to participate in the event to show that people are reaching out to the youth of his town. As I took pictures, I saw how distraught these young men were. They were trying to trust André and his friends and believe in what André was trying to do for them. There was hardness, sadness, and guardedness on their tired faces. Some had trouble standing due to a lack of food. They were quick to fight with each other. At one point, Monique had them sit down and listen to André explain how he wanted to help them. Some of the young men looked at André and Monique with a longing to believe someone. Some looked angry with disbelief. They all seemed extremely weary and without hope.

Later, I asked Monique what the difference was between the youth who were part of the workshops and these street kids. Monique answered that the street kids that André was working with came from a different district. I was shocked. Clearly, there were many differences. The youth that was part of the ministry smiled, sang, and danced. They had jobs that gave them dignity. They had a meal provided for them every day. They ate with each other, sang with each other, and had devotions together every workday. This was family. As I worked with them, I saw their love and concern for each other. Where they once had no one, no food, and no home, they now had food, clothing, family, and a God they were constantly learning about.

The differences between these two sets of street kids were vastly different. It was such a contrast and a picture of beauty that was revealed to me. The power of God was transforming these lives. He was using Monique in powerful ways.

CHAPTER THIRTY-EIGHT

So That . . .

When I first met Monique, it had been four years since her accident in 2004. During those four years, she had set about helping, loving, working, creating, caring, meeting, planning, and more for those people she had come to love. If she had a health concern, she went back to the States and got the issue resolved. I was impressed with her attitude of working and doing whatever she could. In a more recent conversation with her, she shared that some issues were going on in the ministry that needed serious attention. It was a tough situation, and she knew she was the one who needed to deal with it. She explained the situation with a broken heart and then ended the conversation by saying, "Well, I'd better get dressed . . . meaning do not ignore the armor . . . the war is on." She believed there was no use getting upset about situations. God has given us the armor to go through each battle. It is better to just get dressed and start walking.

She had been through more than the normal battle wounds of life. She knew how to get dressed, put on the armor, and face each battle. She always continued to work, plan, and love. She was very human and cried over the hurts and pains of those she worked with. There were times when she wondered if the decisions she made were the best ones. And she always asked, "Do they honor God?"

Time after time, she shared with me that it was in those desperate moments that she felt God's presence. Was she lonely? Yes. But she knew God was there and carried her in those hours. She struggled when she heard that her friends were retired and enjoying their families. "Is that what I should do?" she asked God. Each time, she believed that God had her in Africa for a reason.

I heard her talk to groups in the United States and share her suitcase story. "When you pack for a trip," she said, "you take what you think you might need. All the experiences that life makes available to you are the experiences that will help you down the road. In my case, it's much farther down the road. But I can look back and see how he has used each experience to help another person in their walk through life. I never would have thought that losing a fiancé would have ever come to some good or that having your childhood home bombed would be helpful in some way. But when you are open to allowing God to use you, he can also use your heartaches, joys, pains, accomplishments, and experiences to bring glory to himself."

People often asked her, "When are you going to retire?" Her response was always the same. "I don't see the word *retire* in the Bible. I will continue to serve him until he takes me home." Somehow, I always believed that.

Throughout her life, Monique lived out of that suitcase God had packed for her. She was truly just passing through because she knew her real home was with Christ. She continued to bring His will "on earth as it is in heaven" (Matt. 6:10). Was she beyond what most of us are as humans? I can vouch that she was not superhuman. We laughed and cried together. We prayed together when there were difficult decisions to make. We were silly and stayed up too late talking about all the things our hearts wanted to share. What I saw that set her apart was her desire to not focus on herself. If she saw a need, she got on it.

She shared with me that all the good, the bad, the difficult, and the joys are given to us so we can be authentic in sharing who God is. We are all on a journey, and it's nice to have that comfort from others who will point us in the right direction. We can know we are not alone on this journey of life but that others have gone before us and can help ensure there will always be a rising hope. I am privileged to have met Monique so I can carry on no matter what. I hope you find that encouragement as well. We don't have to have it all together or live a perfect life to reach out to other travelers on their paths through life. We can use our experiences to reach out so the journey becomes bearable and points others to our God.

CHAPTER THIRTY-NINE

It's Time to Get Dressed

Throughout the years I spent with Monique and the ministry in Uganda and Rwanda, many changes took place. When Monique got an idea to help people, she prayed and asked God to either let it happen or stop it if the idea was not from him. The workshops ministered to many marginalized youths. They made greeting cards, wove baskets, made woodcarvings, created imigongo art, fashioned jewelry, and sewed items such as purses and bags to sell. The workshops also worked with widows to grow sunflowers, and then the young men pressed the seeds for oil.

Another aspect of the workshops was helping the community. The woodworking and construction department made screened windows and doors and installed them in impoverished homes to cut down on cases of malaria. They built toilet seats so people did not have to squat over a hole. All these projects helped restore dignity to people in very poor areas near the workshops.

Through partnerships in the United States and Europe, the ministry was able to get sweatshirts for the youth. It can get very cool in the evenings, and if someone has malaria, they get quite cold. The sewing shop made uniforms for school children who could not go to school if their parents were too poor to afford the required uniform. The project was a win-win-win-win situation. Children in the States donated money to the project. The first win was that children in the States learned to care for others as they learned about situations around the world and became empowered to help someone else. The second win was the workshop workers who most likely were not able to attend school and were now being paid to make uniforms for children. The third win was that workers handed out the uniforms, blessing others, knowing they would never be able to go to school. The fourth win was the child in Rwanda who was able to go to school because they received a uniform. It was a beautiful thing to see these young adults blessing others because they had been blessed.

The first youth who showed up at a Youth Might meeting in the 1990s are now older and have a life of their own. Some of them got married and had families. We started bringing wedding dresses to Rwanda so the young brides could have beautiful dresses for their big day. Many of the brides could not afford gowns, so women in the States donated their gowns to these young brides.

The stories I have shared in this book are just a few examples of people who have interacted with this ministry. There are many more stories such as the traumatized youth who the ministry rescued from a mental institution. Now he is married, is a father, is working, and helps with the ministry from time to time.

There are only a few stories about women since they find it more difficult to share their stories, but their stories are not any less important or transformational. Some of the young girls were helped in their schooling and are now teachers, pastors, and workers. Many have married and have children. All their stories have the handprint of God on them, demonstrating His love for them. These young women radiate life as they carry on the love of

God in their lives and their communities. They are now helping others because they were able to receive the help they needed.

Not all the lives Monique came in contact with had a positive outcome. There were numerous times that she was taken advantage of financially, and working with the government seemed to be counterproductive. Promises went unfulfilled, and some of the youth she cared for returned to their destructive ways. Those youth broke her heart, but she knew she must put on the armor and walk on. God loves all these people, and even though God used her as the messenger, the message was not always received. That often made her feel discouraged and doubtful. Those were the times she would say it was time to get dressed, put on the armor of God, and keep walking.

* * * * *

Since my first trip to Africa in 2008, I have witnessed God working in small, quiet ways as well as big, wondrous ways. I have also been aware of how evil has worked to destroy lives and good plans. So many times, in so many ways, I have seen the orchestration of how God uses people to bring his will on earth as it is in heaven in Africa. And Monique demonstrated well how important it is to focus on what God, not Satan, has done. It is a choice we all must make.

Throughout Monique's life, God had his hand on her. In her darkest times, God used others to reach out to her. Once she was in a stable place, she could see how God was there and encouraged her little by little to put her trust in him. We all have a choice to put our trust in God even when we feel we cannot trust. Little by little, Monique's faith grew where she was able to put on the armor and start walking—all the way to Africa.

Monique never claimed to have it all together. One thing I witnessed in her time and time again was that she saw people for who they were. The culture may have been different than what she was used to, but she didn't allow her personal preferences to keep her from getting to know the people in their world. Her faith in God and care for others lived out in front of these vulnerable, frail people, and God took it from there. All praise belongs to God.

The journey of a little girl that started in war-torn Europe, continued in America, and ended up in Africa was filled with blessings and great difficulties. As Monique told me the stories of her life, she connected the dots of how God used an event in one point of her life so that she would be seasoned for something later in her life. She recalled how many times she was able to relate to and care for people who had suffered loss or tragedy.

God does not only use people who have suffered greatly to serve people who are hurting. He can use all of us, for nothing goes unnoticed by a loving Creator. Monique learned when it was time to get dressed, put on the armor, and get walking, her Creator was always right there walking with her providing the hope necessary to walk on.

Epilogue

The last trip I made to Rwanda was in 2019. I didn't have my usual three weeks to invest in the sweet people I had met there and teach them English, so I planned to work the entire nine days to finish up this book and make sure all the information was correct. Monique and I had worked on this book for years, and it was almost finished.

Sadly, that was also the last time I would see Monique. As we finished our work together that year, Monique became ill and couldn't return to the United States. And then the COVID-19 pandemic broke out. We called, emailed, and texted but were restricted to remain in our respective countries. Throughout the summer of 2020, she told me to keep working on the book and that she was ready for the story to be completed and published. She struggled throughout the writing of the book to publish it since so many of her struggles were very personal and she feared what others would think once they knew about the intimate parts of her life, her failures, her struggles, and her pain. Her whole purpose in telling her story was so others who had similar struggles would be encouraged by God to know he loved them no matter what. I talked to her in late July 2020, and she was ready for the book to be published.

August came around, and I returned to teaching in the States in the most difficult teaching year due to the pandemic. In Butare, Rwanda, Monique had fallen and hurt her lower back. She was too weak to come back to the States to get the treatment she needed.

In an email, she told me she was too weak and in too much pain, and asked me to pray that she would not be forced to get on a plane to the United States. Her prayers were answered. On September 2, 2020, Monique was called home to heaven. Her work was finished, and she could finally retire in the arms of her God. She was 89½ years old and worked to serve others up to her dying day. Of course, the pandemic prevented any of us from traveling to her funeral. Her ministry family in Rwanda organized a beautiful funeral for her in Butare, Rwanda.

I felt frustrated that I could not be there to attend her funeral. This woman had meant so much to me and had shown me how believing in others could transform lives. I knew Monique was okay without all the fuss of people at her funeral making a big deal about who she was. Maybe this was another gift God had granted her at the end of her life. She would have been happy with the sweet ceremony the few leaders in the ministry put together to honor her.

As I mourned her death, I decided to take what she lived out in front of me as a gift and a challenge for my own life. I know that is what she would have wanted. What is also amazing is that the leaders decided to carry on her legacy and continue the ministry in what is now known as the Nanny Monique Organization. At first, the leaders were not sure what to do, especially during all the shutdowns during the pandemic. And then the mayor of the district where the workshops were held came and asked the leaders if they could continue the ministry Monique had been doing until the pandemic shut it down. The mayor shared how Monique's work had had such a positive impact on the community and felt it was important to have the workshops operating.

How beautiful that the leaders of the community understood the impact of Monique's work and wanted the work to continue even though she was no longer living. God prepared Monique during her life so she could pass on to the leaders of the ministry the skills to love and care for others. And that is just what was happening.

Our lives are made up of one experience after another. Monique understood that our experiences are given to us so we can walk beside others as we journey through life. Her life exemplified what Desmond Tutu said: "Hope is being able to see that there is light despite all the darkness." Her life was not easy. Our lives are not easy. But we are each given the opportunity to use our experiences to learn and grow and encourage others, so hope may rise. The many people whose lives Monique touched were encouraged by her. Now it is our turn to encourage others with our experiences so God may be praised and others will come to know him. May hope continue to rise.

Acknowledgments

This book began years ago as Monique began telling me her story. The book finally came together after years of writing and rewriting as Monique continued to tell me bits of her story only to scrap it or ask me to reword it. It finally came together and is now a published book. The transforming power of God was evident in Monique's life, and her story was worth telling. Now it is complete.

I want to thank the people I met in Africa who permitted me to use their own stories of transformation. Your stories bring glory to God as witnesses to the transformative power of a living God.

I am so grateful for the people at Lucid Books who worked with me to put my writing into a published book. I could not have done this without their professionalism and care to make sure they captured the essence of my writing. Thank you!

Last but not least, I am so thankful for my family who put up with my years of travel to Africa every summer, listened to the stories that gripped my soul, and supported what consumed my heart. My husband not only encouraged me to pursue my heart but willingly supported me emotionally, spiritually, and financially. Thank you!

May hope rise as God continues to transform lives through life's tragedies and triumphs.

About the Author

Rebecca Sanford was born in Colorado, raised in Arizona, and returned to Colorado with her husband where they raised their two daughters. She received degrees in education along with further training in Bible from Bible colleges in England and Arizona. Currently she holds a doctoral degree in education and is working in the public school system in Colorado. Rebecca has traveled extensively to countries in Europe, England, Asia, and Africa.

Throughout her adult life, she has assisted people by volunteering with refugee programs, short-term missions, and conference speaking along with her husband. While inquiring about a ministry in Uganda and Rwanda, she met Monique Ladosz, and that had a significant impact on her life. Rebecca ended up helping with the ministry for 12 summers.

Rebecca and her husband regularly visit their daughters and grandsons who also live in Colorado. She loves to travel, read, learn new things, and be with her family.